# Lives of the Saints: St. Francis of Assisi and St. Teresa of Calcutta

# Table of Contents

Lives of the Saints: St. Francis of Assisi and St. Teresa of Calcutta 1

Table of Contents 2

Introduction 9

Beginnings 14

Francis Renounces the World 21

Francis's First Followers 27

The First Franciscan Community 33

Life at the Portiuncula 39

Political and Religious Developments 45

Clare of Assisi, Part I: Choosing Christ 51

Clare of Assisi, Part II: A Holy Heroine 57

The Third Order of Franciscans 62

Francis's Encounter with the Sultan 68

St. Francis's Love of Nature 74

The Stigmata 81

Lady Poverty 87

The Death of Francis 92

St. Anthony of Padua 97

The Franciscan Impact on the New World 102

The Franciscan Spirituality of the Pope 113

The Importance of St. Francis for Our Time 118

St. Teresa of Calcutta 126

Introduction 127

Chapter Two: Her Father's Death and the Turn Toward Religion 137

Chapter Three: Mother Teresa's First Religious Calling 143

Chapter Four: Voyage to India 150

Chapter Five: Mother Teresa's Teaching Years 159

Chapter Six: Mother Teresa's Second Religious Calling 166

Chapter Seven: The Origins of the Sisters of Charity 174

Chapter Eight: The Early Days of the Sisters of Charity 181

Chapter Nine: Mother Teresa's First Trip Abroad 192

Chapter Ten: The Sisters of Charity Go International 199

Chapter Eleven: The Muggeridge Interview, Film, and Book 206

Chapter Twelve: The Nobel Peace Prize and Other Awards 216

Chapter Thirteen: Mother Teresa and the Crisis in Beirut 222

Chapter Fourteen: Mother Teresa's Involvement in Other Global Crises 229

Chapter Fifteen: Mother Teresa and the AIDS Crisis—the "New Leprosy" of the West 236

Chapter Sixteen: The Teachings of Mother Teresa and the Sisters of Charity 243

Chapter Seventeen: Mother Teresa's Legacy and Beatification 251

Conclusion 258

**Thank you for downloading this Wyatt North eBook**

Never miss a free book from Wyatt North, and receive FREE inspirational eBooks for your eReader!

Thousands of readers have already joined. Sign up for free today.

Click here for free eBook offers!

© Wyatt North Publishing, LLC 2020

Publishing by Wyatt North Publishing, LLC. A Boutique Publishing Company.

"Wyatt North" and "A Boutique Publishing Company" are trademarks of Wyatt North Publishing, LLC.

Copyright © Wyatt North Publishing, LLC. All rights reserved, including the right to reproduce this book or portions thereof in any form whatsoever. For more information please visit http://www.WyattNorth.com.

Cover design by Wyatt North Publishing, LLC. Copyright © Wyatt North Publishing, LLC. All rights reserved.

Scripture texts in this work are taken from the *New American Bible, revised edition*© 2010, 1991, 1986, 1970 Confraternity of Christian Doctrine, Washington, D.C. and are used by permission of the copyright owner. All Rights Reserved. No part of the New American Bible may be reproduced in any form without permission in writing from the copyright owner.

## About Wyatt North Publishing

Starting out with just one writer, Wyatt North Publishing has expanded to include writers from across the country. Our writers include college professors, religious theologians, and historians.

Wyatt North Publishing provides high quality, perfectly formatted, original books.

Send us an email and we will personally respond within 24 hours! As a boutique publishing company we put our readers first and never respond with canned or automated emails. Visit us at www.WyattNorth.com.

# Introduction

While St. Francis of Assisi is one of the most beloved saints in history, the relevancy of St. Francis for our times in light of the election of Pope Francis has yet to be explored. This book is written with the intention of filling that gap. While it is biographical in nature, it also freely explores themes that relate to St. Francis but are not a part of his life. This book is about more than the life of St. Francis of Assisi; it is about the impact this beloved saint has had through his imitation of Christ, his love of poverty, the Franciscan movement, and his profound influence on Pope Francis.

This book explores classic spiritual themes across the centuries, from medieval Europe to the modern world. In some parts of the book, the geopolitical landscapes are vastly different from our world today, but the problems facing humanity are extremely similar because of our fallen human nature, which is always in need of reform. Here is where the genius of St. Francis comes into play. The enduringness of the spirituality of Francis is no accident but, rather, is based on the attractiveness of Christ as portrayed in the Gospels. St. Francis's call is essentially a call to return to the basics of Christianity. It is a call to Christians to reach back to their roots so that their spiritual lives can draw strength from the pure waters of the Gospel instead of being choked by manmade traditions and worldly concerns. In the words of G. K. Chesterton, the coming of Francis "marked the moment when men could be reconciled not only to God but to nature and, most difficult of all, to themselves. ... his whole function [was] to tell men to start afresh and, in that sense, to tell them to forget" (124).

This same theme can be found in the message of Pope Francis today. He insists that only by returning to the Gospel are Christians able to be faithful to the call of Jesus. Pope Francis recognizes the profoundness of St. Francis's message and has signaled his intent to align his papacy with the message of the *poverello* from Assisi. In an age when the poor are getting poorer and the rich are getting richer, and in which globalization has the potential to bind human beings more closely together, the call of St. Francis is more relevant than ever. Christians in the world must not turn a blind eye to the suffering of so many millions of people today, many of whom are dying of starvation. As Jesus indicated, we must attend to the needs of the poorest if we hope to be shown mercy on the Day of Judgment.

Another theme that will be addressed is the relationship between St. Francis and nature. St. Francis was an ardent lover of creation and took literally the evangelical injunction to preach the Gospel to all creation (Mk 16:15) to the extent that he even instructed the birds to praise their creator. Francis's life was in harmony with God, with his fellow human beings, and with the rest of God's creatures. With the disregard for the natural environment that many people have today, the call to seek harmony with creation is of the utmost importance. This is why St. Francis of Assisi was declared the patron saint of the environment.

Finally, this book investigates the theme of holiness and a deepening spirituality. What made Francis so holy? How might we begin to follow in St. Francis's footsteps so as to become closer to God? St. Francis, inflamed with love by the seraphim, the flaming angel of God, serves as a model for all to follow, not only religious. His call is the call to simplicity and to evangelical perfection, but this is simply the call of Jesus that is addressed to everyone. After all, Jesus instructed his disciples to be perfect as God the Father is perfect (Mt 5:48). For this reason, we have to open our ears to what the spirit of God is saying to the churches and to us (Rv 2:29). By imitating St. Francis, who imitated Jesus, who is the image of the invisible God (Col 1:15), we are able to draw closer to the Father and to become icons of the Father to all who come in contact with us. This kind of spiritual imitation is scriptural since St. Paul asked the Corinthians to imitate him as he imitates Christ (1 Cor 11:1). By way of this mimesis, therefore, we are able to become imitators of God and to spread his goodness to all of creation. Of all the imitators of Christ, St. Francis offered perhaps the most famous approach, which features poverty, simplicity, and flaming charity. May this account of the legacy of St. Francis inspire many to follow Christ more closely.

Come Holy Spirit, enter the hearts of your faithful, and enkindle in them the fire of your love.

Send forth your spirit, and they shall be created, and you shall renew the face of the earth!
Amen.

# Beginnings

In 1181 or 1182 was born one of the most beloved Catholic saints of all time, St. Francis of Assisi. He was born Giovanni di Pietro di Bernardone to Pietro di Bernardone and Pica de Bourlemont. Pietro was an Italian merchant, and Pica was a French noblewoman. Although Pica baptized him Giovanni (John) while Pietro was away on a business trip, when Pietro came back, he became accustomed to calling him Francesco ("the Frenchman"), and the nickname stuck.

Assisi was a small city during the time of St. Francis, with a population of no more than two or three thousand. His family was counted as being in the top-third tax bracket of Assisi, and Thomas of Celano, one of St. Francis's earliest biographers, describes him as coming from an exceptionally wealthy family.

Although Francis was not learned, he was intelligent. He picked up French, most likely during business trips with his father. In fact, he knew French well enough to hold a conversation, sing songs, and write poetry, which he loved. He was also familiar with Latin. Francis acquired knowledge of accounting through his apprenticeship in his father's business when he was about fourteen years old.

St. Bonaventure, the Franciscan professor at the University of Paris who was a contemporary of St.

Thomas Aquinas, describes the coming of St. Francis in dramatic words:

> *In these last days the grace of God our Savior has appeared* in his servant Francis. ... He *preached* to men *the Gospel of peace* and salvation, being himself *the Angel* of true *peace*. Like John the Baptist he was appointed by God *to prepare in the desert a way* of the highest poverty ... he was also assigned an angelic ministry and was totally aflame with a Seraphic fire. Like a hierarchic man he was lifted up in *a fiery chariot* ... he came *in the spirit and power of Elijah*. (Bonaventure, 179-181)

This passage clearly manifests the esteem St. Bonaventure had for his spiritual father, St. Francis.

Yet, Bonaventure makes clear that, initially, Francis had not been yet been captured by Christ. Bonaventure remarks that when Francis was a young man, he "was distracted by the external affairs of his father's business and drawn down toward earthly things by the corruption of human nature" (Bonaventure, *The Soul's Journey Into God; The Tree of Life; The Life of St. Francis*, 187). Francis was the leader of a group of boys from wealthy families, and his generosity gave him the reputation of being prodigal. During this time, he also exhibited an intense aversion to lepers, which he later overcame.

When he was twenty-two years old, Francis joined a militia as a result of a dispute between Perugia and Assisi. Since he was able to afford a horse, Francis avoided service as a foot soldier. Assisi and its allies fought against Perugia, but unfortunately for Francis, he and his friends were captured and put in prison for about a year. He was released in 1203, but life in prison took a toll on his health. Moreover, he had experienced war and had seen his friends killed in battle.

Despite this episode, Francis signed up for a new military expedition in 1205. He had a dream about spoils piled high, and when he asked for whom these riches were intended, he heard the reply that they were for him and his men. Taking the dream literally, Francis thought that it meant he would be victorious in battle. Later on, however, he dreamt that he heard a voice asking him whether it was better to serve the master or the servant. When he replied that it was better to serve the master, he was asked, "Then why do you serve the servant?" Disturbed, he confided in a friend, telling him that he was no longer interested in the military because of that dream.

Francis was twelve miles away from Assisi at that time. He sold his goods, including his horse, and walked back to Assisi. When he was two miles away from Assisi, he spent the night at the church of San Damiano, originally a Benedictine priory, which was in sore need of renovations.

The next day, Francis returned to Assisi. There he found no joy in the life he had lived before. His friends noticed that he was a different man than the jovial youth who had funded their lavish parties. Rather than enlivening his friends, he was somber and pensive. Francis ceased attending such parties and stopped working at his father's business. Francis had been changed by his experience of war.

Not finding peace, Francis made a pilgrimage to Rome and prayed at St. Peter's tomb. He threw a large sum of money at the tomb and traded clothes with a beggar, after which he began to ask for alms. He wanted not only to give alms, but wanted to see what being poor was like. What did it mean to walk around, depending on the charity of others? What kind of life would this be like? This was an important step in what was to culminate in Francis's pure embrace of Lady Poverty. After making his way back to Rome, he began to stay and pray frequently at the church of San Damiano, to which he eventually became attached as a penitent.

Before this occurred, however, Francis began caring for lepers, whom he had previously feared.

Leprosy, a horrific disease that literally eats away at people's flesh, often leaves lepers horribly disfigured. Francis, however, filled with the strength of God, ministered to the lepers, finding in them the presence of Christ. By serving the lepers, Francis realized that he was serving Jesus himself. On top of this, he was moved with genuine compassion and love toward these individuals, whose disease, though causing their flesh to rot, could not diminish their inherent human dignity. They too deserved to be loved and cared for despite their hideous appearance. He decided to live with the lepers and to care for their physical and spiritual needs by dressing their wounds, bathing them, and treating them with respect.

What can we say of this beginning in relation to Pope Francis? Pope Francis is ethnically Italian, as was St. Francis. Jorge Bergoglio was born in 1936 in Buenos Aires to Italian immigrants. Furthermore, both suffered extreme sickness in youth. When Bergoglio was twenty-one, he had a serious case of pneumonia and a part of his lung had to be removed. Both men came from fairly large families, at least by today's standards: Bergoglio was the oldest out of five children, and Francis was one of seven. It seems that the illnesses, trials, communities, and orientations to poverty of the two men affected their spirituality, albeit in different ways, and helped to shape their later lives and characters.

# Francis Renounces the World

Francis was drawn to the humble church of San Damiano that he had visited on his way back from his second short-lived military expedition. There, in the midst of fervent prayer before the crucifix, Francis heard a voice tell him to repair God's house. Francis joyfully consented, thinking that renovating the church of San Damiano was his mission. He rushed back to Assisi, gathered money and supplies, and returned to San Damiano. The priest at San Damiano was skeptical that Francis was serious about restoring the church. Francis began rebuilding the church with his own hands, determined to fulfill his divine quest. He was savvy enough to realize that his father would be furious when he found out that Francis was using his money to repair a church, so he prepared a cellar or a crypt in which he could hide when his father eventually came to look for him.

After several weeks, however, Francis mustered enough courage to go back to Assisi. When he arrived in the city, he was greeted with scorn and ridicule since he looked like a madman. Upon hearing the commotion and discovering that Francis had come back, Pietro sent his men to apprehend his son and had him locked in the cellar of his house. It was only when Pietro left for his annual business trip to France that Pica, Francis's mother, let Francis go. Francis went back to San Damiano.

From a business perspective, Pietro's actions seem to be somewhat warranted. After all, he was a wealthy merchant, and Francis was entitled to half of his mother's dowry. Although Francis's brother was an adept businessman, Pietro could not count on Francis, whom he feared would squander his portion of the inheritance on renovating the church at San Damiano. It was bad enough that Francis was frittering his inheritance away; now Francis was the butt of jokes among the townsfolk, thus rendering him a blemish on the family name. These developments were detrimental to the family's prestige in Assisi, which for Pietro was intolerable.

Upon returning and finding out that Pica had released Francis, Pietro summoned Francis to court. At first, Francis was summoned by the secular consuls. Being astute, Francis claimed that since he was an ecclesiastic, the secular law did not have jurisdiction over him. When the bishop summoned him, however, Francis willingly left San Damiano and went to meet his father and the bishop, who urged Francis to give his father his property and his money. Francis willingly gave up his right to the dowry, stripped himself of his fine clothes, and placed the money on top of the clothes, saying that he wanted to call God his father, rather than Pietro. The bishop then took Francis under his mantle, and Pietro went on his way.

Now Francis was entirely free of worldly cares. With God as his father and with no possessions, Francis set out to start a new life. Of course, it not entirely new; after all, he still had to finish rebuilding the church of San Damiano. How was he to renovate the church, though, without any money?

Francis had an ingenious solution. In what G. K. Chesterton describes as an inverted parable (42), instead of begging for bread, Francis begged for stones from passersby. With these stones, Francis began rebuilding the church of San Damiano. He labored drudgingly with the stones until he completed his project. Stone after stone, he repaired and reconfigured the church of San Damiano. Could Francis have realized at this time that his call was not, primarily, to rebuild a physical church but rather to build up the universal Church of God? This is exactly what Francis's vocation was—to build up the church of Christ, which had fallen into ruins. Francis's charge was to reinvigorate the Lord's people by calling them back to repentance, as if he were a second John the Baptist.

Once finished with his original project of renovating the church of San Damiano, Francis continued his architectural endeavors by repairing the church of St. Mary of the Angels at the Portiuncula. In addition to these two churches, Francis also repaired a church that was dedicated to St. Peter. The fact that Francis worked on rebuilding these three churches has been attributed all sorts of symbolisms by Francis's biographers. What can be said beyond the shadow of a doubt is that these rebuilding projects served two functions: the first, to fulfill literally the call of God to Francis to rebuild his church; and the second, to foreshadow Francis's rebuilding of the universal Church, which was also in need of repair.

What is the state of the universal church today? Is it in shambles? That would be an exaggeration; however, the Catholic Church is reeling from the sex abuse scandal that rocked the Church around the turn of the millennium. Sadly, the wicked deeds of a small percentage of priests and the subsequent cover-ups by several bishops have had a profoundly negative impact on the perception of the Catholic Church. Compounded with this, the ethics of the Church, especially in relation to sexuality, are accused by others of being antiquated and off the mark. In the Western world, where religion is more and more frequently the target of atheistic verbal attacks, the Catholic Church is often ridiculed and mocked. At the same time, there are signs of growth, especially in third-world nations of Africa and South America, and elsewhere in the Southern Hemisphere.

Is it a coincidence that Pope Francis is the first pope from the Southern Hemisphere? Demographically, it is no surprise, despite the fact that he is the first non-European pope since Pope Gregory III in 741. Pope Francis recognizes that, in many ways, the Catholic Church is experiencing multiple crises and is in need of a radical renewal. For this reason, he has called on Catholics to go back to the simplicity of the Gospel message and to follow Jesus. Christians must enkindle within them the flame of God's love and spread the Gospel throughout the world; and the only way they will be successful in this endeavor is to imitate Christ, which was St. Francis's sole goal in life. By dedicating themselves to serving Christ and imitating him, Christians will be able to serve the poor, thus being true disciples of Jesus Christ. In this age of globalization and capitalism, such Christianity is more necessary than ever.

# Francis's First Followers

Francis's *modus vivendi* from around 1206 to 1209 was to repair his churches, to care for the lepers, to beg for his daily food, and to pray before the crucifix. He did not expect to start a movement or to live in a community with anyone. Francis was an itinerant—a sort of penitent freelancer, if you will. For this reason, he was surprised when two men met him, wanting to imitate his way of life.

The first man who intended to follow Francis was Bernard of Quintavalle, a wealthy young man. After speaking to Francis in 1208, he literally sold everything he had and gave his money to the poor. After this, he joined Francis and imitated his life of prayer and penance. At nearly the same time, a man named Peter joined them. He was an older man who was poorer than Bernard had been. These two men, in contrast to the other citizens of Assisi, decided to follow Francis even though he appeared to many to be out of his mind. They perceived the movement of the Holy Spirit within Francis, a humble man who would eventually catch the world on fire with the love of Jesus and the simplicity of the Gospel.

Now that Francis had brothers, he wanted to receive ecclesiastical approval for his way of life. There was one problem, however. Both Don Peter, the priest at San Damiano, and Bishop Guido were absent for some reason or another. In order to get advice on what he should do, Francis went into Assisi with his two brothers and approached the parish priest of the church of San Nicolò di Piazza. He asked the priest to perform a *sortes biblicae*, a practice in vogue at the time that consisted of opening up the Bible three times and receiving a commentary by a clergyman as to what God was telling an individual through the Scriptures. Francis thereby hoped to gain insight into God's will for him and his companions. In response, the priest opened up the missal to the following three passages: Mark 10:17-21, Luke 9:1-6, and Matthew 16:24-28. Taken together, these three scriptural passages portray a radical way of life and eventually formed the basis for the entire Franciscan rule. The three men carefully memorized these texts and kept them ever before their hearts.

After this encounter, Francis and his companions lived together for about a year. Francis still did not have approval for his way of life, although he had been given guidance as to what it should be. Since Don Peter and Guido were still away, he became determined to acquire approval by going to Rome. Francis and his companions therefore undertook a several-day journey to Rome. At the Lateran, they unexpectedly met Bishop Guido, who was upset that these men were seeking a way of life from the pope instead of going through him first. After explaining to Guido that their intentions were sincere and that they were only striving to do the will of God, Francis managed to acquire Guido's assistance.

Guido's contact in the papal court was Cardinal John of San Paulo Colonna. Cardinal Colonna most likely regarded Francis's motley crew as merely another of the many religious movements that were cropping up at this particular time in medieval Europe. The cardinal gave a hearing to Francis and his brothers but advised them to join another established group. Perhaps he thought their intention was to be hermits. In the end, the cardinal agreed to bring their case before the pope.

Cardinal Colonna presented his case to Pope Innocent III, most likely without Francis and his two companions in attendance. According to St. Bonaventure, Innocent had a dream that Francis was holding up the Lateran basilica and was keeping it from collapsing. This certainly would explain the quick acceptance of Francis's rule. After accepting their little rule, the pope gave the men his apostolic blessing and told them to preach penance and to increase in numbers, thus constituting the group as one of lay preachers. This was a surprising turn for the brothers. Francis had no aspirations to preaching, although he was passionate about penance. He and his companions were tonsured, a sign that they were officially men of the Church and had authority to preach.

Francis, however, was not known as a preacher. In fact, there is a saying attributed to him that Christians are always to preach the Gospel, but to use words only when necessary. This saying sums up rather well his attitude toward preaching: one's way of life, rather than words, was to be one's primary testimony of Christ.

Before the men left, Francis had a dream that a giant tree stood in front of him. As he approached, he began to grow to such an extent that he was able to bend down and place his hand on the tree. Recalling this dream to his brothers, Francis believed that it applied to them since the pope had listened to Francis's request. After visiting the tomb of the apostle Peter, they made their way back to Assisi, no doubt filled with joy but also harboring some uncertainty as to what their new way of life was actually calling them to do.

Francis's at having been received by the pope and at having his proposal approved so quickly must have been similar to the emotions Jorge Bergoglio experienced upon being elected to the Chair of Peter. Cardinal Bergoglio surely wanted reform in the Church and sought a holy successor to Benedict XVI, but that he should be elected pope? He did not see this coming. In humility, however, he stepped out on the balcony to the people, greeted them, and asked for their blessing. No man elected pope has all of the answers laid out before him as to what is going to occur after his election. A pope must resort to his advisors and must ultimately rely on the inspiration of the Holy Spirit to help guide him in guiding the Church of Christ.

This is a situation that every Christian experiences to a certain degree. Even when one makes the decision to dedicate one's life to Christ, the way is often imperfectly clear at first. This experience, however, goes a long way in keeping the Christian humble enough to recognize that he or she relies on God for spiritual progress. May the Holy Spirit always enlighten us so as to help us discern what we ought to do.

# The First Franciscan Community

Accounts among St. Francis's biographers concerning the accruement of his first followers differ. Some, such as St. Bonaventure, suggest that he had quite a following before he went to Rome to seek the approval of Pope Innocent III for his way of life. According to Bonaventure, Francis had twelve followers, a highly symbolic number as the number of the twelve disciples of Christ, before he sought the papal blessing.

One of these initial followers, a priest in Assisi named Silvester, initially abhorred Francis's way of life, but then had a dream. As Bonaventure recounts,

> [Silvester] saw in a dream the whole town of Assisi encircled by a *huge dragon* (Dan. 14:22) which threatened to destroy the entire area by its enormous size. Then he saw coming from Francis's mouth a golden cross whose top touched heaven and whose arms stretched far and wide and seemed to extend to the ends of the world. At the sight of its shining splendor, the foul and hideous dragon was put to flight. (Bonaventure, *The Life of St. Francis*, III.5)

Upon having the dream three times, Silvester told Francis and his followers about the experience and began to follow the friars in their way of life.

It is said that Francis sent out his followers two by two, in accordance with the Gospel injunction (cf. Mk 6:7), to various places throughout Italy. Their home base was the Portiuncula, where they met together after these preaching missions. True to their rule, the friars followed a stringent way of life that included penance and charity. The purpose of these excursions was to preach penance to the people and to increase the numbers of the Franciscans, who were not called Franciscans at the time; instead, Francis told his brothers that they were to call themselves "penitents from Assisi." Taking no food, water, or extra clothes, they preached in various places, such as the Marches around Ancona and Florence. In fact, Bernard and Giles traveled as far away as France and Spain, visiting Santiago de Compestela. Wearing no shoes and enduring the cold, Bernard gave away his hood to a beggar. It took Bernard and Giles months to make the journey to Spain and back. Not knowing the language, Bernard and Giles could not preach to the people in these foreign lands and were often despised by the people.

These primitive excursions did not yield a large following, but they served as an excellent means for scouting out sites for future houses. In all of the places these early Franciscan friars visited, there are

Franciscan sanctuaries today. The daring of these early Franciscans, and their willingness to risk all for the sake of Christ, planted the seeds for the future development of the Franciscan order.

On their way back from Rome, Francis and his companions took up residence in a dilapidated cowshed about forty miles north of the city. There they prayed and grew as a community. This humble abode sheltered the friars from the elements. Since they had no place to pray privately, Francis built a reed hut as an oratory. The friars prayed intensively in the morning and evenings. They listened to Bible readings, prayed the Lord's Prayer and the Hail Mary, and prayed from the Psalms. It is said that Francis prayed so intensely that one night, one of his brothers saw a fiery chariot rushing around the shed rafters. He at once notified the other friars, who all saw it and believed that it was the soul of Francis praying.

The preaching of Francis and his friars had a profound effect on the populace of Italy. They did not often receive permission to preach in churches, so they preached in the open air in the language of the people, rather than in Latin, which the people could not really understand. This contrasts with the practices of such saints as St. Bernard, who preached primarily in Latin to the educated. Francis, on the other hand, was dedicated to preaching the good news to the poor. The people were inspired by Francis's recounting of biblical scenes, such as the nativity or the crucifixion, and were entertained by his examples of morality and immortality from Arthurian romances. As a troubadour, Francis had acquired considerable storytelling skills and even a talent for entertainment. His enthusiasm brought about many kinds of reconciliation, including the reconciling of parish priests and parishioners, rich and poor, and many others of unequal social status. Francis taught people to view all others as their fellow brothers and sisters in Christ, and he inflamed many with the love of God.

Because of the success of their preaching, Francis and his companions attracted more followers. Eventually, Francis realized that the cowshed could not accommodate all of the friars and that they would have to find another place to stay. His prayers were answered when the Benedictines gave Francis and his companions the use of the Portiuncula as their headquarters. From there, the Franciscans would be able to preach penance to all and to multiply in numbers, ushering a myriad of souls into the kingdom of God through a life of penance, humility, poverty, and holiness.

Pope Innocent III expressed his hope that the Franciscan friars could serve as examples to his bishops and priests, who often liked to live in luxury and were frequently more concerned about their own comfort than the state of their flock. While Francis certainly set an example for the clergy, his preaching of penance had a profound impact on the common people. Likewise, the reformation of the Catholic Church today cannot be merely a reformation of the clergy; instead, all Catholics are called to follow in the footsteps of Christ. Jesus is calling all Catholics to enkindle within themselves, through the Holy Spirit, a newfound devotion to his Cross and to serving others. Without the conversion of heart among the people of God, Pope Francis's reform will not be successful. Now is the time when we need to open our hearts to God's grace; now is the time of salvation!

# Life at the Portiuncula

St. Mary of the Angels, popularly called the Portiuncula, was a substantial gift to Francis and his companions. Francis loved this new place for a variety of reasons. The simplest reason for Francis's affection for this chapel was its dedication to the Blessed Virgin Mary. In medieval Europe, there was a burgeoning of Marian devotion. Francis had always associated Our Lady with poverty, and he maintained a dedicated devotion to her.

At the Portiuncula, Francis's companions grew in faith. Although these men were not highly educated, they learned about their faith through intense prayer and service. Their learning was acquired by studying not books but the Crucified. This disposition is reflected in St. Bonaventure's answer to St. Thomas Aquinas, his Dominican colleague at the University of Paris, who had asked the Franciscan where he had acquired his learning. In reply, Bonaventure pointed to a crucifix. This kind of learning was more closely aligned with pathos than with book learning as such, and Francis's companions grew considerably in this kind of knowledge and faith.

What were the friars' days like at the Portiuncula? Francis and his brothers prayed the Church's liturgical prayers, including the Mass, at which Francis would serve as deacon. Their senses were caught up in the Mass, and their prayers arose to God with the incense.

After Mass, the brothers would perform their chores. Mindful of the importance of prayer, Francis made it a part of his Rule that the friars were not to speak from morning until noon. After noon, talk was not to be idle but, rather, to concern holy or necessary things. At the command of Francis, the friars would also go out and preach sermons at various churches in the area; and if they were invited anywhere, they would eat what was offered to them.

As the order grew, Francis acquired a keen insight as to the natures of those who intended to join his order. Occasionally, a rotten apple would slip past him, but he was always able to determine when this had happened. One man who expressed an interest in joining Francis had sold everything but then gave his money to his family instead of to the poor. When Francis found out, he dismissed this man from the order.

Masseo was tested by Francis to see if he was worthy of being allowed to stay in the order. Although Masseo had a remarkable ability to preach, Francis was concerned that this would make him prideful. Therefore, Francis assigned Masseo to such menial tasks as cooking and gatekeeping. Finally, his fellow friars protested, asking for a redistribution of the chores. All the while, Masseo kept silent and performed his duties obediently. This convinced Francis of his sincerity and his virtue. From that point on, Francis often chose Masseo as a companion and used him as a messenger.

What distinguished Francis and his companions from the Benedictines was the itinerancy and mendicant charism of the former. Rather than staying confined to one place, the Franciscans were often on the road, preaching to the people and serving the poor. In this sense, the Franciscans could be described as nomadic. Their travel was structured on a rotational basis; some of the friars were sent out to certain places to preach, whereas the other friars stayed at the Portiuncula to pray. Their style of preaching was not concerned with doctrine; instead, their focus was on encouraging people to embrace a life of penance and to rely on the sacraments. Francis and his companions eventually acquired some of the homiletic techniques that were in vogue at the time, but at first they preached simply the love of Jesus and the necessity to convert to the Lord. They always taught more by example than by their words. Through their itinerant nature, Francis and his companions were able to scatter the Word of God to the people, not in the form of a sophisticated exegesis but as living, walking icons of Jesus Christ. In Francis, people saw the face of Christ and a disciple who was wholly devoted to living the message that Jesus proclaimed.

The Franciscans were also a mendicant order. Instead of living off of endowments or tithes, as the Benedictines often did at the time, the friars grew their own food and often had to resort to begging for alms so that they could acquire enough sustenance. This aspect of their lives was something Francis insisted upon because of the radicalness of the Gospel injunction to give up everything and follow Christ. Ultimate poverty was Francis's goal, not for the sake of being poor but, rather, for the sake of following Christ as closely as possible. He firmly believed that by taking the leap of faith and doing what God asked of him and his companions, they would be provided for; and he was not disappointed.

All Christians are called to put on Christ by tenaciously fulfilling the demands of their baptism. We are all called to be Christ to others. This is a message that is just as true today as it was in thirteenth-century Italy. A Christian conversion comes about by living a life that is in conformity with Christ's, which allows people to begin seeing Christ alive in us. This is the kind of conversion Pope Francis wishes for the Church—a conversion that is capable of bringing about joy to people in today's somber world. Only by knowing and proclaiming Christ are Christians capable of reclaiming for themselves the joy that is rightfully theirs, a joy that stems from knowing they are loved by God.

The itinerant nature of the Franciscans was also a blessing since this initial impulse to spread the Gospel throughout the surrounding villages was a sign of greater things to come. In 1492 Christopher Columbus, a Secular Franciscan, sailed to the Americas. In 1493 Friar Juan Perez, a Franciscan, celebrated the first Mass in the New World. In the eighteenth century, Blessed Junípero Serra, O.F.M., set up multiple missions in California and was instrumental in the development of that portion of the present-day United States. The Franciscans played a vital role in the history of the Americas, a role they would not have been able to fulfill without the primary example of Francis and his followers. We will explore this theme further, later in the book. For the time being, we will continue the story of St. Francis himself.

# Political and Religious Developments

At the Portiuncula, with its celestial architecture and peaceful aura, the friars certainly felt peace. During this time, however, the world was not so irenic. A crusade raged in the Holy Land. Otto, the new emperor, had a falling out with Pope Innocent III, and was ultimately excommunicated by him. In a fortuitous set of circumstances for Assisi, Otto moved against Perugia for supporting Philip of Swabia and the pope, so he had the prisoners from Assisi released from the Perugian prisons. Brothers and fathers were reunited with their families after years of imprisonment. Otto also forced Perugia and Assisi to make peace and oversaw the signing of a treaty at Assisi in 1210. The people of Assisi were elated at this fortuitous turn of events.

In addition to the upswing in the political state of affairs, there was a growing religious fervor. In 1212 the location of St. Rufino's relics was made known to a priest in a dream. After consulting with Bishop Guido, it was decided that the relics would be placed with great ceremony beneath the altar of the new cathedral. This led to many miracles and increased the esteem of the bishop in the eyes of the people.

In 1211 or 1212, Francis decided that he should travel to the Holy Land to seek peace between Christians and Muslims and thereby halt the bloodshed resulting from the Crusades, even if doing so meant that he would be martyred. With another friar, he went to the Adriatic coast and set sail on a ship toward the Orient, but a storm prevented them from reaching their destination. They arrived on the other side of the Adriatic instead. Unable to find a vessel willing to carry them, they stowed away on a ship, bringing with them a generous supply of food that someone had left them. When another storm broke out and the sailors began to run out of food, Francis and his companion shared their food with the sailors. The ship landed on the western coast of Italy, where Francis and his companion made his way home. Although his plan was thwarted this time, Francis would ultimately journey to the Holy Land in 1217.

When Francis arrived back at Assisi, many men and women were eager to follow his way of life. The women of the town and of the surrounding cities were impressed with Francis's genuineness, his love for the poor, and his desire to serve the people of God. Many sought his counsel. One woman sought his advice about her cantankerous relationship with her husband, who occasionally took to beating her. His response was that she should not worry but, instead, go home and strive for salvation with her husband. When she returned home, the two reconciled and lived the rest of their lives in celibacy, eventually dying on the same day. Their neighbors described the couple as saints.

Giacoma de Settesoli, one of the richest women in Italy at the time, assisted the friars. She contributed to the their good works and was present at Francis's death. After this event, she moved to Assisi, where her remains are kept partway down the stair to St. Francis's tomb. The eagerness of women to help Francis and his companions evokes images of women in the Gospel who contributed to the apostles' purse. Without the assistance of such women, Jesus' and Francis's respective ministries would not have been as successful as they were.

Women are extremely important in the Catholic Church, whether they are nuns, mothers, or single women. Through their affection, support, prayers, service, and generosity, women take a prime place in the cultivation of good works and in fostering the faith. Along with mothers, fathers share an obligation to hand on the faith to their children and to live as models of holiness for their children to emulate. This is all the more necessary today, when the family, the basic unit of society, is under attack.

According to Pope Francis, the role of women in Christianity is made most apparent in the mother of Jesus. In the pope's own words, "The woman has the gift of maternity, of tenderness; if all these riches are not integrated, a religious community not only transforms into a chauvinist society, but also into one that is austere, hard, and hardly sacred" (Bergoglio, 102). Women sustain the community through their sensitivity and their loving concern for all. There is a need for the feminine aspects of Christianity to be highlighted once again and for women to rediscover and embrace their feminineness.

In the pope's view, the philosophy of feminism, as characterized by radical feminists who insist on bridging the gap between the sexes, has failed to bring about true good to women. After the women's suffrage campaign of the 1920s, radical feminism attempted to draw battle lines between men and women. While Pope Francis insists that the philosophy of feminism does not benefit women, he is aware that women have "been the object of use, of profit, of slavery, and ... relegated to the background" (103). He calls this the work of Satan, who desires to crush the sources of life and salvation.

Pope Francis desires for men and women to recognize that masculinity and femininity are different but complementary and that there ought to be no gender-based power struggle in the Church. As Pope Francis notes, the mother of Jesus was greater than the apostles, but the ecclesiastical authority was passed on to men (102, 104). In *Evangelii Gaudium*, Pope Francis states,

"The Church acknowledges the indispensable contribution which women make to society through the sensitivity, intuition and other distinctive skill sets which they, more than men, tend to possess. ... we need to create still broader opportunities for a more incisive female presence in the Church" (sec. 103).

May Mary, the mother of Christ, intercede for the Church, and may men and women everywhere open their hearts to the specific, engendered roles God has given them within the Church. Only through such an acceptance of the distinctions and respective grandeur of each of the sexes will Christians adequately support one another, and the role of the family be safeguarded.

# Clare of Assisi, Part I: Choosing Christ

One of the women who followed St. Francis as a result of his growing renown was Clare of Assisi. Clare was born in either 1193 or 1194 to an aristocratic family. She grew up during a turbulent time; during Clare's childhood, Assisi was embroiled in the same local wars in which Francis engaged as a soldier. In fact, at the time of her birth, several houses next to her family home had been burned down.

Typically, aristocratic girls were brought up quietly, confined to the women's quarters as their families prepared them for marriage to a wealthy suitor. Little did Clare's family know that their daughter would become a great saint and cofounder of a religious order. According to the reports of her friends, Clare was a pious and modest child. She kept herself hidden whenever her family had male guests, and she saved her food so that it could be distributed to the poor. She was fond of romances and had a devotion to St. Agnes, who had rejected the suitors her family had wanted her to consider. Incidentally, one of her friends was named Ginevra, after Guinevere.

Having heard some of Francis's sermons on Sundays in 1210 or 1211, Clare became enamored of the poor man's message. She yearned to find out what impelled Francis to seek the way of life he did and why he had followed the words of Christ so literally. However, she faced a dilemma: since she was sixteen at the time, it would have been socially unacceptable for her to speak privately to Francis, who was in his late twenties by now. What was she to do? She had to act quickly since her family was pressing her to marry. Her case was made all the more urgent by her recent acquisition of a sizable dowry.

Somehow, a secret meeting was arranged between Clare and Francis. For the sake of propriety, Bona di Guelfuccio served as a chaperon to Clare while Brother Philip the Long accompanied Francis. A number of such clandestine meetings occurred, during which Francis urged Clare to embrace a life of penance. Ultimately, Clare was convinced that in order for her to fulfill God's plan for her, she would have to devote herself to Christ entirely as a nun. The question remained as to what kind of nun she would become.

Clare decided on a bold course of action, probably with the help of Francis and Bishop Guido. First, she gave her dowry away. Naturally, this upset Clare's family and her suitor, who still encouraged her to marry him. Despite the pressure from her family, she refused. Finally, on Palm Sunday in 1212, Clare received a palm branch from Bishop Guido, somehow bypassing the women's line. According to legend, this was a sign that had been established beforehand between Clare, Francis, and

Bishop Guido. In the evening, Clare slipped out of her family's house through a secret passageway that was covered with bricks and beams. Obviously, Clare's family was not fond of the idea of their daughter entering a convent.

After she successfully snuck out of the house, Clare was met by a handful of people, including Francis, possibly another friar, and perhaps Pacifica, her mother's cousin. They went through the woods and made their way to the parish church, where Clare exchanged her gown for a simple habit, promised obedience to Francis, and made a vow of poverty. Francis cut her hair as a sign of his acceptance. Clare was finally a Franciscan, but she could not live with the Franciscan friars for several reasons. A woman living with friars would have been perceived as a scandal; and, moreover, her family could have found her easily if she had stayed with Francis and his brothers. For this reason, the decision was made that Clare would go to San Paulo delle Abbadesse at Bastia, which lay a short distance from Assisi.

When Clare's family found out that she had escaped and was at the Benedictine monastery, seven of them rode there to retrieve Clare. After several days of threatening and enticing her, they finally surrounded her in the chapel. Clare clung to the altar, but it was only when she showed them that her head had been shaved that they realized there was no hope of convincing her to return with them. After this, they left Clare.

Shortly after this, Francis moved Clare, Pacifica, and her sister Catherine, who had also been accepted into the order, to San Damiano. Thus was the first convent of Franciscan sisters established. This was also, perhaps, one of the last gifts of Bishop Guido to Francis, since the bishop died later that year.

Clare and her sisters needed a rule of life, which she requested that Francis compose for them. This rule proved similar to that which Francis had written for his brothers. Whenever anyone suggested that Clare become a "normal" nun by joining an abbey, she always replied that she had made her vow of obedience directly to Francis. Furthermore, her rule marked her as a Franciscan.

While some biographers report that something of a romance existed between Clare and Francis, nothing improper is apparent in their relationship. While it is true that they had many similarities, their mutual affection was based on their admiration for each other's devotion to Christ. For this reason, the friendship of Clare and Francis stands as a pure model of platonic friendship based on a common love of Christ. Clare admired Francis's devotion to Christ and was inspired by his particular form of imitating Christ; otherwise, she would not have eventually chosen that particular lifestyle. Nothing surprising in this is surprising since Christ is supremely attractive and all who follow him become as he is. This is why the saints shine in resplendence and why the saints have influenced so many others.

While their friendship lasted for as long as Francis lived, Clare and Francis hardly met after she was settled in San Damiano. They regularly corresponded, however, and their friendship and affection for each other never grew stale. What makes their love all the more edifying is that they were always true to their vows to Christ and never mistook the beauty of God himself for the beauty of the other person.

# Clare of Assisi, Part II: A Holy Heroine

Throughout medieval Europe in the early thirteenth century, thousands of women were joining convents and religious orders. This often afforded women—especially those who were on the margins of society, such as the poor and the widows—a safe haven where they could be looked after. Of course, most of these nuns' intentions were spiritual rather than monetary, and they were overall sincere in their motives for joining these orders. In this cultural context, the women's branch of the Franciscan order experienced its initial burgeoning.

It is said that some six years before Clare joined the Franciscans and established the second order, Francis declared that San Damiano would be a house for holy women. Clare and her sisters therefore had a place to stay, and her group of companions slowly increased. Clare went on to outlive Francis by nearly three decades. Within her lifetime, she was able to see the spread of her communities over much of Europe. She advised popes and became known as a protector of Assisi. Clare's influence, which was influenced in turn by Francis's example, was nothing less than profound, and this rippling effect spread across the known world.

Clare's way of life was similar to that of the Franciscan friars in that both the men's and women's branches of the order were strictly devoted to a life of poverty.

Therefore, they depended solely on almsgiving rather than on endowments, lands, or other typical sources of income to which other orders, such as the Benedictines, were accustomed. At the same time, Clare recognized early on that it would not be prudent for her sisters to beg in the streets for food as the friars did. As a result, they accepted food if it was offered, but they primarily stayed in their convents. Francis therefore arranged for two friars to beg for food on behalf of Clare and her sisters. This way, Clare and her companions could remain true to their vow of poverty and live a true mendicant lifestyle while avoiding danger and scandal.

Clare and her companions lived a simple life. They met several times a day for prayer. Silvester and Leo, two Franciscan friars, heard the sisters' confessions and said Mass for them. Clare kept her sisters busy by directing them to make their own habits, grow fruits and vegetables, and help out their neighbors. The simplicity of their way of life must have struck a chord with many of the women in Assisi and its environs. Within several years, over fifty companions joined Clare. Soon after this, with the establishment of other convents, their numbers grew into the hundreds.

At the end of Clare's life of prayer and penance, a dozen of the original members of her order testified to her sanctity, including her sisters Agnes and Beatrice, her cousins Balvina and Amata, Pacifica, Benvenuta, Christina di Bernardo, and Agenese di Oportulo. Clare's companions offered strong testimony to her holiness. In one account, Pacifica described how Clare often healed the sisters simply by praying and making the sign of the cross. Benvenuta described Clare's bravery when Arab mercenaries had scaled the convent walls.

G. K. Chesterton observes that if Clare had eloped instead of running away from her home to become a nun, the modern world would regard her as a heroine. At the same time, she is to be considered among the greatest women in the history because of her bravery, sanctity, and determination. Chesterton also defends Clare's early decision to run away from home, observing that at that particular time in history, girls were married at an early age and teenagers often went to war, started businesses, and made other adult decisions. Therefore, at seventeen, Clare was certainly capable of making the decision to join an order. Having made this choice, Clare became a source of inspiration to thousands of others who followed in her wake. Of course, all of this was due to her connection to Francis and, ultimately, due to Francis's particular imitation of Christ.

The chaste friendship of Clare and Francis remains one of the most remarkable friendships in the history of

Christianity. Dante and Beatrice, John of the Cross and Teresa of Avila, Francis and Clare—these spiritual couples, so to speak, complemented each other in remarkable ways. In fact, it is almost impossible to mention one without the other, so intertwined were the lives of these individuals. Francis looked upon Clare as a daughter and a confidant, as a disciple and as a unique spiritual contributor to the direction of the Franciscan movement since only she could directly watch over the women in her community day in and day out. Clare made Francis's way of life accessible to women as well as to men, thereby opening up the Franciscan movement to both genders.

What about those people who lived in the world, however? Would they be barred from following the Franciscan way of life? The next chapter explores the origins of the Secular Franciscan Order. With the establishment of this lay order, the Franciscan triumvirate of orders would be complete.

# The Third Order of Franciscans

In Cannara, a village approximately six miles south of Assisi, Francis preached a sermon on penance that so impressed the villagers that everyone wanted to leave and follow him. Surprised, Francis told the villagers to be patient and that he would let them know the best way for them to be saved. This was the beginning of the Secular Franciscan Order.

Francis's advocate, Cardinal Ugolino (later to become Pope Gregory IX), aided Francis in composing of the rule of the Third Order. Thereafter, men and women, regardless of their stations, could join the Franciscan movement by living in the world and infusing it with the Franciscan charism. They took vows and met together frequently to pray, but they also continued to perform the daily duties attendant to their respective states of life. By 1215, many men and women were associated with Francis's movement by way of belonging to the First, Second, or Third order.

There are no written records of this earliest period of the Third Order of Franciscans, who at that time were simply called the Brothers and Sisters of Penance. We know that there were many followers of Francis from all walks of life. Francis urged them to honor the church, go to confession regularly, attend Mass, respect the clergy, love their neighbors and enemies, give alms, be abstemious, and avoid sin.

Some of Francis's most valuable contributions came from early tertiaries. The wealthy count Orlando of Chiusi donated Francis Mt. LaVerna as a retreat site in 1213. At Mt. LaVerna, Francis would receive his vision of the seraph and, eleven years later, the stigmata. Giovanni di Velita gave Francis a sanctuary at Greccio. There many tertiaries gathered to pray psalms and hymns. The number of tertiaries soon numbered in the hundreds, if not thousands. The influence of the Third Order rapidly became apparent.

In addition to the influence that the Third Order of Franciscans exerted during the time of St. Francis, they have since had a profound impact on world history. There is a long list of renowned secular Franciscans, including popes, cardinals, royalty, adventurers, writers, artists, musicians, and scientists.

Among famous popes, Pius IX, Leo XIII, St. Pius X, Bl. Pius XII, and St. John XXIII were secular Franciscans. Pius IX is known for having put the seal on the doctrines of papal infallibility and the Immaculate Conception, whereas Leo XIII is known for his social encyclicals and devotion to Our Lady. Of course, St. John XXIII was known as the pope who began the Second Vatican Council and was canonized (along with St. John Paul II) on April 27, 2014. St. Charles Borromeo, a cardinal, was also a secular Franciscan.

There have also been royal members of the Secular Franciscans, including St. Louis IX, St. Elizabeth of Hungary, St. Elizabeth of Portugal, and Ferdinand and Isabella of Spain. Speaking of the latter, Christopher Columbus too was a secular Franciscan, as was Vasco de Gama. St. Joan of Arc was also a Franciscan tertiary. These leaders and explorers did much to advance the modern world and to institute justice for all people, especially the poor. Without Ferdinand and Isabella, Columbus could not have set out on his world-changing quest.

Dante Alighieri, the famous Italian poet who wrote the *Divine Comedy*, was a Franciscan tertiary, as was Miguel Cervantes, the author of *Don Quixote*. Giotto di Bondone, the Florentine painter who portrayed the life of Francis in paintings, was another secular Franciscan; so were Leonardo da Vinci, Raphael, and Michelangelo, the great Renaissance artists. Giovanni Pierluigi da Palestrina, the talented composer of sacred polyphony; Franz Liszt, the debonair pianist and composer; and, in our own times, John Michael Talbot are all associated with the Secular Franciscans. Some of the greatest artists who have ever lived were devotees of Francis's way of life and desired to emulate the ideals of the poor man of Assisi. Francis's aesthetic sensibilities, manifested in his love of nature and his appreciation of all God's creation, as well as his love of God through his imitation of Christ, inspired numerous artists in his wake. Francis of Assisi has thereby inspired some of the greatest works of art and literature the world has ever seen.

In addition to those Secular Franciscans who were associated with the humanities, a number of scientists were Franciscan tertiaries. These Franciscan scientists included Galileo Galilei, the great astronomer and inventor of the telescope; André-Marie Ampère and Luigi Galvani, who were instrumental in the field of electricity and electromagnetism; and Louis Pasteur, who saved countless lives through his work on vaccinations. Without these scientists, the world as we know it would not exist. Obviously, nothing in the spiritual vision of Francis would impede learning or knowledge. Although Francis exhorted his brothers to be simple and not to seek learning for its own sake, the vocation of the tertiaries to follow their own callings and occupations in this world allowed for these scientists to foster their faith and their scientific work simultaneously, thereby bringing much benefit to humanity by way of electrical and medical technology.

This impressive list demonstrates just how influential the Secular Franciscan Order has been since St.

Francis's life. For many great leaders, artists, scientists, and other visionaries, devotion to Christ in the form of a Franciscan lifestyle was the religious inspiration behind their lives and work.

# Francis's Encounter with the Sultan

Once Francis had settled Clare and her sisters and had established the Brothers and Sisters of Penance, he decided that it was time for him to preach to the Sultan in hopes of brokering a peace between Muslims and Christians. Bonaventure and Thomas of Celano insist that Francis was bent on martyrdom. This is perhaps overly dramatic since Francis's primary intentions were to speak to the Muslim leader, preach the Gospel, and bring about peace between Christians and Muslims—although, if this meant that he would have to die for his faith, then so be it.

Francis set out in 1219 and sailed to Acre in the summertime with perhaps ten or eleven friars. One story has Francis letting a child choose which friars would go, since the captain would not accept more than a dozen because of a lack of space. When Francis reached the Crusader camp, he found a motley crew of warriors, including knights as well as common foot soldiers. The Crusaders made their way to Damietta, a city on the delta of the Nile in Egypt. At some point, either before or after the Christian victory over Damietta, Francis went to speak to Malik-al-Kamil, the caliph, with Brother Illuminato. They were in danger of death since there were bounties for the heads of Christians. When the soldiers realized that Francis was no threat and that the friars, who looked like madmen, might prove entertaining to the sultan, they brought them to al-Kamil.

Once in the presence of the sultan, Francis was graciously received, and he was allowed to spend a few days preaching to the sultan's court. Some accounts have Francis offering to endure a trial by fire if a Muslim in the court were willing to do the same, to prove the relative veracity of their respective faiths, but the sultan refused. There is no reason to think that Francis was mad for making such an offer. As Chesterton noted, "Indeed throwing himself into the fire was hardly more desperate, in any case, than throwing himself among the weapons and tools of torture of a horde of fanatical Muhammadans and asking them to renounce Muhammad" (102).

There are those who believe that Malik-al-Kamil was a member of the Sufi brotherhood, which emphasized union with Allah through love. If this was the case, and he was in fact a mystic, it would help explain why Francis was not treated with contempt and ignominy. Something more than Francis's unassuming appearance, derived from his beggar's clothes, seemingly made an impression upon the sultan. Francis preached to the sultan and to his theological experts, who unanimously declared that Francis and Illuminato were dangerous and that the sultan should behead them immediately for tempting them all to commit apostasy. Of course, the sultan did no such thing. Instead, he listened patiently to what Francis had to say. When they were done speaking, the sultan explained that it was impossible for him to convert but asked Francis to pray for him and to ask God that he would show him the true faith before he died. He then offered Francis and Illuminato a treasure, which Francis refused. Instead, he accepted a sumptuous meal that the sultan provided, and the brothers were then escorted back to the crusader lines.

This encounter had a profound spiritual significance. Francis made a favorable impression on the clerics from Acre, some of whom became Franciscans. Moreover, Francis had attempted something no other Christian had done: to approach a Muslim with the Christian faith, without bearing arms. His outreach to Muslims occurred during a time when five of his brothers were martyred in Morocco, where they had preached the Gospel of Christ, an event that inspired St. Anthony of Padua to join the Franciscans.

Risking his own life to preach the Gospel and bring about peace, Francis demonstrated missionary zeal and a willingness to accomplish great things through his Christian courage, which eventually led to Franciscan custody of the Holy Land. In 1229 the Franciscan friars had a house near the fifth station on the Via Dolorosa. In 1309 they settled in the Holy Sepulcher and Bethlehem. Finally, in 1342, Pope Clement VI decreed that the Franciscans would be the official custodians of the sacred sites for the Catholic Church. This custody over the Holy Land still exists today, as the Franciscans have maintained a presence in the Middle East over the centuries. There is a nearly ubiquitous presence of Franciscan friars at the holy places of Jesus' life, death, and resurrection.

In today's world, as in Francis's, Islam is a force to be reckoned with. Since September 11, 2001, the dangers of radical Islam have become apparent to the entire Western world. The imperative to preach the Gospel has not lessened since the time of Francis, although in our contemporary world, an emphasis is placed on interreligious dialogue. Francis's desire to bring about peace and his zeal to save souls must be rekindled in the Church today.

Pope Francis recently traveled to the Holy Land in company with a rabbi and an imam. This symbolic gesture represented Pope Francis's dedication to peace, religious tolerance, and openness to people of different views. At the same time, the pope called on Muslims not to offend the name of God by committing violence in God's name. Christians must stand firm in their faith;

they must respect Muslims but also preach to them through the example of extraordinarily holy lives. Only by following the path of Christ will the peace that this world so desperately needs become a reality.

# St. Francis's Love of Nature

Augustine Thompson, O.P., a recent biographer of St. Francis of Assisi, describes Francis's love of nature as follows:

> Francis felt a deep union with living creatures, who, like the lilies of the field and the birds of the air, lived the Gospel precept of complete reliance on God spontaneously and naturally ... they followed the Gospel of complete reliance on God better than some of Francis's followers. Here was a "religious community" that needed no leader and no correction. No wonder Francis felt a union with them. (54)

Francis's love of nature is made evident by the legends that surround his interaction with animals. Once he found a cricket at the Portiuncula and asked it to sing its praises to God. Every day for a week, the cricket would sit on his finger and sing for him for an hour, until he gave it permission to leave. On another occasion, he walked into the middle of a flock of birds and told them to praise God. They began to open their wings and sing, which delighted Francis greatly. This theme of creation praising God is a powerful image, for it highlights the unity that exists among all God's creatures.

In addition to his love for creation, Francis had a soft spot for animals that were in danger of being killed for food, even if it was intended for Francis and his brothers. Once, when a brother had caught a hare to feed the community, Francis petted the animal and let it go out of compassion. Francis had a special affection for lambs in particular since they reminded him of Christ, the Lamb of God. Seeing a couple of lambs being carried to the slaughter by a shepherd, he convinced the shepherd to trade them for his cloak. Francis liked larks above all other animals because they reminded him of his Franciscan brothers, with their beautiful singing and their habits like the lark's feathers. His love of animals was so great that he cared for the worms by moving them out of the road so that they would not get crushed.

A wolf once terrorized the villagers of Gubbio. Francis approached and rebuked the wolf, but he recognized that it attacked the villagers' animals because it was hungry. He made a pact between the wolf and the people, telling the villagers that if they promised to feed the wolf, it would not attack them or their animals. The villagers agreed, surprised to see the wolf acting so benignly toward Francis—even shaking Francis's hand with its paw. After two years, the wolf died, and the villagers buried him in their church. Indeed, beneath the chapel of San Francesco della Pace, a skeleton of a wolf was excavated in 1872.

Francis's relationship with nature is easily romanticized. While he loved creatures, however, he also described a bird that had drowned as cursed and believed that some pests were sent by the devil to make him suffer. He did not like flies, and whenever a brother did not work, Francis was wont to call him Brother Fly. He playfully referred to his stubborn body, which he attempted to tame and rule, as Brother Ass.

Although Francis loved creatures dearly, he was not a vegetarian. He followed the Gospel rule that permitted disciples of Christ to eat meat. Nor was Francis pantheistic; rather, he recognized clearly that creatures came from God but were not God himself. Francis always distinguished between the Godhead and the rest of creation. However, he did somehow narrow the gap that existed in the medieval mind between human beings and animals—by associating with them, speaking to them, asking them to praise God, and emphasizing the common creator of both humans and beasts.

In addition to his affinity for animals, Francis loved all of creation. He loved flowers and cared for trees. In fact, he would ask the brother who was in charge of cutting wood to be sure to leave enough trees that they would grow again. His love of all creation is perhaps best expressed in his "Canticle to Brother Sun," which he composed shortly before he died:

Most High, all-powerful, good Lord,
Yours are the praises, the glory, the honor,
and all blessing.
To You alone, Most High, do they belong,
and no man is worthy to mention Your
name.
Praised be You, my Lord, with all your
creatures,
especially Sir Brother Sun,
Who is the day and through whom You give
us light.
And he is beautiful and radiant with great
splendor;
and bears a likeness of You, Most High One.
Praised be You, my Lord, through Sister
Moon and the stars,
in heaven You formed them clear and
precious and beautiful.
Praised be You, my Lord, through Brother
Wind,
and through the air, cloudy and serene, and
every kind of weather
through which You give sustenance to Your
creatures.
Praised be You, my Lord, through Sister

Water,
which is very useful and humble and precious and chaste.
Praised be You, my Lord, through Brother Fire,
through whom You light the night
and he is beautiful and playful and robust and strong.
Praised be You, my Lord, through our Sister Mother Earth,
who sustains and governs us,
and who produces varied fruits with colored flowers and herbs.
Praised be You, my Lord, through those who give pardon for Your love
and bear infirmity and tribulation.
Blessed are those who endure in peace
for by You, Most High, they shall be crowned.
Praised be You, my Lord, through our Sister Bodily Death,
from whom no living man can escape.
Woe to those who die in mortal sin.
Blessed are those whom death will find in Your most holy will,
for the second death shall do them no harm.
Praise and bless my Lord and give Him

thanks
and serve Him with great humility.
*(Francis and Clare: The Complete Works, 38-39)*

This poem, as simple as it is profound and as plain as it is beautiful, supposedly inspired Dante to write his *Divine Comedy* in Italian instead of Latin. To this day, "Canticle to Brother Sun" is the oldest surviving piece of poetry written in Italian.

In 1979, Pope John Paul II declared St. Francis of Assisi to be the patron saint of ecology. A large part of the legacy that Francis bequeathed to later generations was his example of harmony with creation. Instead of setting themselves over and against creation, and perceiving plants, animals, and the earth as mere objects to exploit, human beings should care for the created world. Francis, who made a habit of calling animals his brothers and sisters, displayed a connection with nature, and sensitivity toward all of creation, that the modern world would do well to emulate.

# The Stigmata

Toward the end of Francis's life on earth, in the fall of 1224, he had a mystical experience while on retreat at Mount LaVerna. Before this incident, Pacifico, one of Francis's companions, had a vision in which he saw a row of thrones in heaven. One of the thrones, which stood higher and was more ornate than all the others, sat empty. When Pacifico asked whose throne this was, the reply came that it had been Lucifer's but would now belong to Francis since what Lucifer had lost by pride, Francis gained by his humility. In accordance with his special devotion to St. Michael the Archangel, Francis decided to precede the feast of St. Michael in 1224 with a forty-day fast on Mount LaVerna. He went with a small group of friars and made his way up the mountain, where he prayed for some weeks with his brothers.

On the feast of the Exaltation of the Cross, September 14, when Francis was engaged in deep meditation, a seraph (see Isa 6:2) appeared to Francis in a vision. Rays that emanated from the seraph pierced Francis's hands, feet, and side, thus leaving the impression of Christ's wounds upon his body. This profound mystical experience left an indelible mark not only upon Francis but also upon the history of the world. Never before had the wounds of Christ appeared so obviously on one of his followers. In fact, Francis's stigmata represented the first documented case of this phenomenon.

Thomas of Celano, one of Francis's earliest biographers, describes the stigmata in the following words:

> He was in a vision a Seraph upon a cross, having six wings, extended above him, arms and feet affixed to a cross. *Two of his wings were raised up over his head, two were stretched out as if for flight,* and *two covered his whole body*. Seeing this, he was filled with the greatest awe, but as he did not know what this vision meant for him, joy mixed with sorrow flooded his heart. He greatly rejoiced at the gracious look that he saw the Seraph gave him, but the fact that it was fixed to the cross terrified him. With concern his mind pondered what this revelation could mean, and the search for some meaning made his spirit anxious. But understanding came from discovery: while he was searching outside himself, the meaning was shown to him in his very self. At once signs of the nails began to appear on his hands and feet, just as he had seen them a little while earlier on the crucified man in the air over him ... His right side was marked with an oblong red scar as if pierced by a lance. (320-321)

This dramatic encounter with a celestial being made a lasting impression not only on Francis but also on his brothers. This impact, however, was not far-reaching until after his death, when his stigmata were revealed to all. Francis only told his closest brothers at Mount LaVerna, including Brother Illuminato, about what had happened, saying that he was told secrets he must not repeat to anyone. Try as he might, however, Francis was unable to conceal his stigmata from everyone since he was already such a popular religious figure.

In Bonaventure's classic account of this event, after Francis received the stigmata, the hailstorms that had so often plagued the vicinity of Mount LaVerna ceased, much to the amazement of the people who lived in the area. Instead, the sun shone, and all of nature was serene. In addition to this meteorological miracle, Bonaventure attributes a number of miraculous cures to Francis's stigmata. On one occasion, Francis touched a poor man who had trouble sleeping in the cold; at once, the man felt a marvelous heat and fell into a deep sleep. Another time, a plague had broken out among the sheep and cattle in Rieti. A man was given a vision to fetch water in which Francis had washed his hands and feet and to sprinkle it on the animals. As soon as the water touched the animals, they recovered.

For the last two years of his life, Francis carried on his person the wounds of Christ. Many people, including Pope Alexander IV, testified to seeing Francis's stigmata while he was still alive. Despite Francis's best efforts, he could not conceal his stigmata from everyone. The wound in his side, especially, caused him great pain, particularly when someone touched it accidentally.

St. Bonaventure's interpretation of Francis's vision is that he received it so that "he might learn in advance that he was to be totally transformed into the likeness of Christ crucified, not by the martyrdom of his flesh, but by the fire of his love consuming his soul" (Bonaventure, 306). In Bonaventure's mystical theology, the six wings of the seraph "symbolize the six steps of illumination that begin from creatures and lead up to God, whom no one rightly enters except through the Crucified" (55). This is the structuring motif behind Bonaventure's *Itinerarium Mentis ad Deum*, or *The Soul's Journey into God*.

What is the meaning of the stigmata for us today? Firstly, they are a reminder of the love Christians should have for Jesus Christ, who was crucified for our sins. They are also a reminder that we should have the passion of Our Lord always before our minds. Christ's wounds express the remarkable love God has for humanity and the gratitude we owe him for his many gifts to us, the most important of which is the gift of salvation. The merits of Jesus' sufferings continue to apply to Christians today. Although he is no longer hanging on the Cross but, rather, is seated at the right hand of God the Father, he still extends his arms over the world. From his throne in heaven, our high priest raises his pierced hands in prayer over the world, interceding for his people until we are made perfect. For this to occur, however, we need to cooperate with the grace that God offers us. He wishes that we would be made perfect, but how few are those who courageously relinquish all else to follow him! The stigmata of St. Francis are a reminder of God's infinite love and of Jesus' triumph over death, in which we are called to share.

# Lady Poverty

Francis described poverty as "the special way to salvation" (Bonaventure, 240). He longed for poverty with all his heart and desired to be the poorest person for the sake of Christ. He fully embraced the Gospel ideal of selling one's possessions and giving them to the poor, and he made this a requirement of entering the order. Whenever he saw someone dressed more poorly than himself, he would rebuke himself and strive to be poorer than the person he had encountered. Francis would not leave the poor person and then strive to be poor by his own means, however; far from this, Francis saw in the faces of the poor an image of Christ himself, to be imitated by grace. According to Bonaventure, Francis told his fellow friars, "When you see a poor man, my brother, an image of the Lord and his poor mother is being placed before you. Likewise in the case of the sick, consider the physical weakness which the Lord took upon himself" (Bonaventure, 254).

Francis tended to the needs of the poor and would even give away his own necessities, which others had given to him. Bonaventure recounts that Francis also took upon his shoulders the heavy loads of poor people so that they would not have to carry the burdens themselves. Francis's compassion shone in all he did, especially in his relationship with the poor. On one occasion, Francis gave away his clothes to a beggar woman, who ran away with them. Finding that she did not have enough cloth to make a dress out of them, she went back and told Francis. He therefore asked his companion to give his clothes to the woman as well, ensuring that the woman would now have enough material.

The friars' eating habits were extremely austere. They often squatted on the ground as they ate. The food they prepared often consisted of scraps of meat, some vegetables, and bread crusts. Whenever a brother soaked beans overnight, Francis would rebuke him since they had taken vows not to have any concerns for tomorrow. Francis was not an ascetic for the sake of increasing his and his brothers' pain but out of his love for Christ. His intention was not to make the brothers suffer; if that had been the case, then he would not have given the best food to the friars who were elderly and sick. When Silvester was ill, for instance, Francis gave him the best grapes from the vineyard before the other brothers awoke. This anecdote reveals that although Francis was an ascetic, he did not revel in pain; rather, he accepted suffering out of love for his crucified Lord.

What was the inspiration for Francis's poverty? Put simply, it was his desire to imitate Christ as closely as possible. He saw Christ's life as one of voluntary poverty that thereby enabled others to become rich. Jesus was born in a manger, had no place to rest his head, and was ultimately executed as a criminal. Francis did not want to be provided for. He did not want to join a monastery where he would have all of the food, clothing, and goods that he would ever need. He wanted to know what it was like to be truly poor, to be a poor person living in the world and to rely on the good will of others for his daily sustenance. Francis wanted to beg for his food, and he wanted nothing in this world to call his own. He wanted only to be like Jesus. For this reason, Francis's vision of poverty was strikingly different from the monastic view of poverty as common possession. Francis, rather, wanted to have no possessions whatsoever.

Francis was so enamored of poverty and so inspired by this Gospel ideal that, according to Bonaventure, Francis called poverty "his mother, his bride, and his lady" (244). He referred to poverty as Lady Poverty and told his friars to "love and be faithful to our Lady Holy Poverty" (*Francis and Clare,* 164). In Francis's vision, Our Lady and poverty are especially linked. Not only was Mary poor, like Jesus, but she was also the exemplar of all the virtues because she was free from all sin and perfectly obedient to Christ. This outlook reflects the doctrine of the Immaculate Conception, which was defended by the Franciscan theologian Bl. Duns Scotus and proclaimed a dogma by Pius IX in 1854. In "The Salutation to the Virtues," which was sometimes called "The virtues possessed by the holy Virgin, and which should be present in a holy soul," Francis addresses the virtue of poverty as follows: "Lady, holy Poverty, may the Lord protect you with your sister, holy Humility" (*Francis and Clare*, 151). This beautiful salutation demonstrates how closely Francis connected poverty with the Blessed Virgin Mary.

For Francis, poverty was a way of sharing in the poverty of the holy family. It was his way of participating in the family of God, relying only on God the Father for his temporal well-being while imitating his Lord Jesus and Our Lady, whom he found to be an indispensable spiritual advocate. It was for this reason that he entrusted his order to her care.

## The Death of Francis

In 1225 and 1226, toward the end of Francis's life on earth, he endured a variety of physical ailments. He already suffered from the excruciating pain of the stigmata, by which he was conformed to the Cross of Christ; now, he would suffer near-blindness, malnutrition, and malaria. In the spring of 1225, Francis went to say his farewell to Clare; but Clare, cognizant of Francis's physical ailments, insisted that he stay with her near San Damiano so that his friars could look after him. She had a house of reeds constructed and attached to the church. There Francis was tormented by sunlight and could not read by candlelight. He could not receive eye surgery right away since it wasn't the proper season; he would have to wait. Francis lived in this hut for almost two months. During this time, Francis composed the "Canticle to Brother Sun." As Augustine Thompson remarks, in this canticle Francis paid homage to the sun, which caused him his greatest pain (123).

In the summer, Francis left Assisi for Rieti to acquire medical treatment for his eyes. His brothers found it difficult to care for him. Although Francis had allowed his fellow friars to eat choice food when they were sick, he refused to eat the best food during his own sickness. He even declined to hear the reading of Scripture, saying that he recalled enough Scripture and could meditate on many verses. He also quoted David, who said that his soul refused to be consoled. For these reasons, Francis proved a difficult patient.

Finally, Francis consulted with a doctor who decided that the best course of action would be to cauterize Francis's flesh from his jaw to the eyebrow of his bad eye. This operation was performed, but it did not have the desired effect of stopping the flow from Francis's eyes. Another doctor recommended that his ears be pierced. This was done as well, also to no avail. The only thing Francis could do now was to recover from his surgeries. Afterward he received medical attention at Siena, but this did not help him much, either.

One evening Francis started to vomit blood, which could have been a result of a stomach ulcer or stomach cancer. Francis began to prepare his brothers for his death and for life in the Franciscan order without him. Brother Elias heard of this and asked Francis to compose a last testament for the brothers.

Finally, in July or August of 1226, Francis returned to Assisi with an escort of armed knights since the people of Assisi feared that he would die in a foreign city. The people of Assisi, who had formerly believed that Francis was a madman, now honored him as a saint even before he died. They placed him in the bishop's house and had an armed guard posted in front of his quarters at night. Although Francis was nearly blind, he was still able to appreciate music, so he asked that the brothers sing hymns of praise. The doctor who assessed Francis at this time told him that he did not have long to live and that he would die between the end of September and October 4.

The friars carried Francis to the Portiuncula on a litter so that they could honor his wish to die there, the place where his order first grew. He blessed Assisi as he left it. When he arrived at the Portiuncula, he called on Giacoma and sent word to Clare. He left his last testament with the brothers and asked them to sprinkle his body with ashes once he died and to say psalms over his dead body. One evening before his death, he could not sleep because of the pain he endured. The next morning, he took bread and had it broken and distributed to the friars who were present. He then blessed the friars and asked them to keep in their prayers all those who had been in their order, were currently in their order, or who would join their order in the future.

Only a few days later, Francis passed. Immediately beforehand, he asked that the passion according to the Gospel of John be read to him. According to Bonaventure, one of the friars saw Francis's soul ascending into heaven in the form of a bright star. It was also reported that larks gathered in a great multitude over the place where Francis lay and that they sang when he died. This sign was fitting since the sight of them filled him with joy and he had so often invited them to praise God.

Before he died, Francis asked the friars to assist him with one last act of humility: he wanted his body stripped of all of his clothes after his death and left in this state for as long as it takes a man to walk a mile, which is approximately thirty minutes. The friars honored Francis's request. Francis was naked when he came into the world and naked after he departed. So committed to poverty was Francis that, at the end of his life, he wanted nothing attached to his body. After the prescribed period of time, Francis's body was clothed in a gray habit. At his death, the miracle of his stigmata was made known to all who were present.

In 1228, two years after Francis's death, Pope Gregory IX declared Francis a saint. This pope was closely connected to the Franciscans. He wrote the rule for the Poor Clares and also heavily influenced the rule of the

Secular Franciscans. For a long time, he had been the cardinal protector of the order, and he personally knew Francis. Since Francis died just after the sun had set on October 3, his feast day was declared October 4, for in the medieval period, the commencement of the new day was recognized at sundown.

Francis's death serves as a model for all Christians to follow. He left the world stripped of every worldly desire, and he focused on the passion of his Lord as he was dying. Francis's death, however, was made all the more pure and holy since he had prepared for it throughout so much of his life by his great devotion to Jesus Christ crucified.

The example he offered to his followers had a ripple effect that impacted the rest of history. This is evident in one of Francis's great disciples, St. Anthony of Padua, who is the subject of the next chapter. Following this is an investigation of the Franciscans' impact on the New World. Thereafter, over the course of two chapters, Francis's legacy on Pope Francis will be analyzed. The final chapter addresses the importance of St. Francis of Assisi for our time.

# St. Anthony of Padua

One of the most famous Franciscan saints in history is St. Anthony of Padua, a Portuguese priest who became associated with Padua after he moved to Italy. His birth name was Fernando Martins de Bulhões, and he was born in 1195 in Lisbon. He hailed from a wealthy family and joined the Augustinians at the age of 15. He learned Latin and theology and became an expert in Scripture. After being ordained a priest, he encountered some Franciscan friars who eventually settled in a hermitage near the Augustinians. Fernando was drawn to their lifestyle. When he heard that some of the Franciscan friars who had gone to preach the Gospel in Morocco had been martyred for the faith, he decided that he wanted to become a Franciscan. He obtained permission to leave the Augustinians so that he could become a Franciscan, and they acquiesced.

Fernando took the name Anthony after joining the Franciscans, after the name of the hermitage of the Franciscans he had first met. Anthony set out for Morocco but had to return to Portugal; the ship he was on, however, was blown off course and brought him to Sicily. He eventually settled in a Franciscan convent in Tuscany. In 1222 a group of Dominicans came to town, but they were unprepared to give a sermon. Therefore, Anthony was called upon to deliver the sermon. Although he was unprepared, he gave a sermon of such brilliance that it left a lasting impression on all who heard him.

Soon afterward, he came to the attention of St. Francis. Although Francis did not want his brothers to be immersed in books or overly concerned with theological arguments, he recognized the necessity of having a theologian in their midst so that those Franciscan friars who had a calling to the priesthood could acquire the necessary theological training. Francis found that Anthony truly loved the Franciscan charism and that his skill as a theologian did not detract from his simplicity, genuineness, and humility. In 1224 Francis put Anthony in charge of teaching all the friars who went on to pursue theological studies. According to Benedict XVI, "Anthony laid the foundations of Franciscan theology which ... was to reach its apex with St Bonaventure of Bagnoregio and Bl. Duns Scotus."

While Anthony was a masterful theologian, he was better known as a preacher. Anthony primarily preached in France and Italy, and his sermons always proved edifying to his listeners. He inspired people to turn away from sin, and criminals would reform upon hearing him preach about the mercy of Christ. Pope Gregory IX referred to him as the Ark of the Testament, and his preaching was described as a "jewel case of the Bible." His preaching ability was renowned throughout much of Europe. His methods included the use of allegory and the explanation of Scripture in symbolic terms. Anthony bequeathed to the church two sets of sermons: "Sunday Sermons" and "Sermons on the Saints." These two collections of sermons were to be used by Franciscan preachers. The richness of his sermons is so great that Pope Pius XII declared St. Anthony a Doctor of the Church.

Exhausted from his missionary journeys and having contracted ergotism, Anthony went with two other friars to a retreat at Camposampiero, a village about twelve miles north of Padua, to get some rest. On their way back, Anthony died at the age of 35 on June 13, 1231, just outside the gates of Padua. He was buried in Padua and quickly became the patron saint of the town. In fact, his canonization process was so swift—the second quickest canonization in the history of the Catholic Church—that he was canonized less than a year after his death.

In art, Anthony is depicted with either a lily or the child Jesus. This latter symbol is derived from several stories wherein Anthony was seen praying in his room, warmly holding the infant Jesus in his arms. He is also known as the patron saint of lost objects. Many Catholics ask St. Anthony to intercede for them when they lose their keys or other objects of importance. The reason for this is that once, when a collection of Anthony's sermon notes was stolen from him, he prayed to God that he might reacquire his book, and the thief, experiencing contrition, returned the book. In some cultures, Anthony is the patron saint of marriages as well since it was said that he reconciled couples.

St. Anthony of Padua was known also as the "Wonder Worker," both during his life and afterward, because of the many miracles attributed to him. In addition to his vast popularity as a miracle worker, he also stands as a prime example of a humble theologian, providing Bonaventure and Duns Scotus a distinctly Franciscan theological basis. Furthermore, Anthony was known as a friend of the poor because of his love for those who lacked worldly wealth. Overall, he exemplified a man who was remarkably influenced by the Franciscan spirit—who united his own talents with the evangelical way of life of St. Francis of Assisi. His charity, fidelity to the Gospel, and humility, which reflect Francis's, have contributed to his popularity among all God's people. May St. Anthony of Padua pray for us today as we strive to follow the will of God in our lives.

# The Franciscan Impact on the New World

As previously mentioned, King Ferdinand and Queen Isabella of Spain, as well as Christopher Columbus, were Third Order Franciscans. The Franciscans were also one of the largest religious orders in Europe at the time. In fact, one estimate places the number of Franciscan friars in 1493 at 22,000. In that same year, Franciscan friars accompanied Christopher Columbus on his second expedition to the Americas. Franciscan priests said the first Mass in the New World at Port Conception on Hispaniola.

In 1523 and 1524, Franciscan expeditions set out to Mexico from Santo Domingo, a Franciscan base. Then, in 1527, a diocese was formed under the rule of Bishop Juan de Zumárraga, a Franciscan. Zumárraga set up the first printing press in the New World. Moreover, he was the bishop of Mexico City in 1531 when St. Juan Diego Cuauhtlatoatzin, better known as Juan Diego, received his vision of Our Lady of Guadalupe, who has since become the patroness of the Americas.

Some friars, in particular Pedro de Betanzos and Francisco de la Parra, became fluent in the Mayan language. In fact, it is partially thanks to these two Franciscans that experts are able to read Mayan hieroglyphs today. By the end of the sixteenth century, churches dotted Mexico and the Franciscans had spread their missionary activity to North and South America.

In 1573, the Franciscans arrived in Florida. By 1675 there were as many as 40 friars overseeing as many as 36 missions in Florida. This, however, was the apex of Franciscan missionary activity in Florida since the conflict between England and Spain over that portion of the New World was heating up. By 1706 the majority of Franciscan missions in Florida were inoperative.

While Texas remained connected to New Spain, Franciscan missionaries spread throughout the area. Some missionaries went so far as to call the vast area occupied by Texas, New Mexico, Arizona, and California "The New Kingdom of St. Francis." In the eighteenth century, 21 missions were established in Texas, operated by more than 160 friars. Thousands of American Indians were baptized during this time.

The Franciscans began their missionary activity in California in 1769. Bl. Junípero Serra founded 21 missions from San Diego to San Francisco. The Franciscan missionary activity in this region led to an estimated 80,000 baptisms over the next century. The work of Junípero Serra was instrumental in the settlement of California.

The Franciscans were also active in the English American colonies. They assisted the Jesuits in

Maryland, New York, Pennsylvania, Kentucky, Michigan, Illinois, and Minnesota between 1672 and 1699.

Many of the Franciscan missionaries gave up their lives for the faith. These martyrs are remembered for their bravery and their fidelity to the mission to spread the Gospel of Christ to the ends of the earth, even at the cost of their own lives. Indeed, without the bravery of such men, America would not be the place it is today.

Franciscan provinces in Europe sent Franciscans over to the United States in the early 1800s. Fr. Michael Egan, O.F.M., an Irish Franciscan, accepted an invitation from Catholics at Lancaster, Pennsylvania, to administer to their spiritual needs. Arriving in 1802, he eventually became the first bishop of Philadelphia in 1808 after Rome received a positive review of Fr. Egan by Archbishop John Carroll. The Diocese of Philadelphia at the time included Pennsylvania, Delaware, and parts of New Jersey. Bishop Egan died in 1814.

In the late 1800s, the Franciscans took charge of parishes and schools throughout the United States. The number of Franciscans steadily grew until the 1960s, when it experienced a decline. American Franciscans typically work in friaries, missions, and schools. Some are academic while others are not. The Franciscans in the United States are dedicated to the poor and the suffering. This is especially true of the Franciscan Friars of the Immaculate, founded in the 1970s, which operates in New York and elsewhere.

In the Americas today, the Franciscans carry with them the example of their spiritual father, St. Francis of Assisi, and strive to emulate his life of penance, dedicated poverty, and commitment to helping the poor. They seek to be a light to others through their holiness and their particular apostolates. The Franciscan impact on the New World was far-reaching and continues to produce positive results among the people of North and South America. The vision of St. Francis and his particular way of following Christ have inspired tens of thousands of Franciscans over the last five centuries since Columbus, a Franciscan tertiary, discovered the Americas. Many cities in the United States—Los Angeles, San Diego, San Francisco, San Antonio—are named after local Franciscan missions. The Franciscans extended the reign of Christ geographically, baptized thousands of people, and helped to settle the New World through their missionary zeal. The life of St. Francis continues to have a profound impact on countless people today, in the Americas and elsewhere.

# The Election of Pope Francis

On February 28, 2013, Pope Benedict XVI announced his resignation as pope. This resignation was the first time a pope had stepped down since Pope Gregory XII reluctantly gave up the papacy in 1415 to end the Western Schism. It was also the first time a pope had willingly resigned since Pope Celestine V in 1294. This completely unexpected move meant that a papal election was inevitable. The conclave met on March 12, 2013, to decide who the next pope would be. The next day, the cardinals elected Jorge Mario Bergoglio, the Archbishop of Buenos Aires, Argentina, who took the name Francis.

The election of Francis was special for many reasons. He is the first Jesuit pope, the first pope from the Southern Hemisphere, the first pope from the Americas, and the first non-European pope since Pope Gregory III in 741. He was also the first pope to take the name of Francis.

The relationship between Francis of Assisi and the popes of his era is apropos of Pope Francis taking up his name. Francis of Assisi received the call to rebuild Christ's church, which was in shambles. Initially, Francis believed that Jesus was talking about the church at San Damiano; later on, he realized that the Lord was referring to the entire Catholic Church. Eventually, Francis made his way to Rome to seek papal approval of his way of life. It is said that Pope Innocent III had a dream that Francis was holding up the papal basilica and that this dream inspired him to accept the rule of Francis's way of life. These facts indicate that Pope Francis, too, intends to be a reformer who seeks to bring about greater simplicity in the church and to stir up the Church's zeal for the poor.

When Francis stepped out on the balcony, he gave an eminently simple impression. Shortly after being elected pope, instead of approaching the people on the steps of a pedestal on the balcony in St. Peter's square, Pope Francis chose to stand on the same level as the cardinals around him. Furthermore, he refused to wear the traditional mozzetta that is usually worn by popes upon their election and instead chose to wear a simple white cassock, with his own pectoral cross rather than a fancier one made of gold. He also decided to have his fisherman's ring made out of silver, not gold. Pope Francis then humbly asked the people gathered in St. Peter's Square to pray over him.

When he received the congratulations of the cardinals, Francis did not sit on the papal throne but accepted their congratulations standing up. Finally, when the evening was over, Francis decided to take the bus back to his hotel instead of riding in the papal vehicle. He decided not to live in the papal residence, either, but to reside in the Vatican guest house instead.

Pope Francis explained that he chose the name Francis because Cardinal Cláudio Hummes from Brazil had told him, when it was clear that he would be elected pope during the conclave, not to forget the poor. This made him think of St. Francis. Pope Francis has expressed great admiration for the saint, saying of him that he "brought to Christianity an idea of poverty against the luxury, pride, vanity of the civil and ecclesiastical powers of the time. He changed history."

The pope's decision to call himself Francis demonstrated creativity, for this was the first time since Pope Lando in 913-914 that a pope had not called himself by the name of one of his predecessors. Even then, Lando was that pope's birth name. One would have to go back to Pope Romanus in 897 to find a pope with an original name that may have been different from his birth name.

The coat of arms of Pope Francis does not explicitly convey his connection to Francis. It is rather simple, comprising the Jesuit symbol, HIS, on a blue field, surrounded by three other prominent symbols: a sun, an eight-pointed star, and a cluster of spikenard. IHS is a monogram of Jesus since it is a reflection of the first three letters of Jesus' name in Greek (i.e., iota, eta, and sigma). The star is a symbol of Our Lady, and the spikenard is a symbol of St. Joseph. For this reason, it could be said that Pope Francis has the symbols of the Holy Family on his coat of arms.

While there are no explicitly Franciscan symbols in Pope Francis's coat of arms, it is possible to derive an implicit connection to St. Francis of Assisi if one uses his or her imagination. The Jesuit symbol of the IHS monogram, inside the sun and the three nails, can be seen as relating to St. Francis of Assisi. The three nails represent the nails that pierced Christ's hands and feet. Francis's stigmata reflected these very wounds of Christ. In fact, his earliest biographers, including Thomas of Celano and St. Bonaventure, claim that there were nails in Francis's hands and feet. As for the sun, recall that toward the end of his life, St. Francis wrote his "Canticle to Brother Sun," the first creature for which he thanks God in the canticle. While it is improbable that the Ignatian symbol was intended to demonstrate this symbolism, there remains an unintentional, implicit connection.

The election of Pope Francis has already had profound effects, even though scarcely over one year has passed since he became pope. The faith of Catholics is reinvigorated; unbelievers are pleasantly surprised; and the media can't seem to get enough of the charismatic pontiff. While the pope is charismatic, it is easy to recognize that he possesses not only a magnetic personality but also, more importantly, the Holy Spirit. May the Lord bless Pope Francis and help him to lead the Catholic Church wisely. The next chapter will explore in detail Pope Francis's Franciscan spirituality.

# The Franciscan Spirituality of the Pope

Pope Francis is, of course, a Jesuit. For this reason alone, Pope Francis's spirituality cannot be entirely defined by the Franciscan charism. At the same time, much can be said about Francis's Franciscan spirituality. His attraction to St. Francis is evident since, after all, he chose to be called after this saint from Assisi; but what is it about the pope's spirituality that is explicitly Franciscan? The pope's Franciscan spirituality rests on three important points: (1) his concern for the poor, (2) his concern for simplicity, and (3) his concern for nature, in the form of environmental advocacy.

Like his namesake, Francis has a deep love of the poor. We have to remember that it was his fellow cardinal's advice to remember the poor that inspired Bergoglio to choose the name Francis. A few days after he was elected pope, Francis declared that he wanted a church for the poor. He wants the whole of humanity to be concerned about the well-being of the poor and to cooperate together so as to care for the needs of those who are suffering the most. This solicitude for the poor is demonstrated by Bergoglio's actions. He celebrated Holy Thursday Mass at a juvenile detention center and washed the feet of youths, including women, something that had never been done before by a pope. He is also touched by the plight of the poor and is said to sneak out at night, dressed in ordinary clerical garments, so as to distribute food to those in need. And what is the reason for Pope Francis's actions? As he expressed it, those who serve the poor serve Christ. Of course, this is an echo of what Jesus himself said in Matthew 25:31-46, in the parable of the sheep and the goats.

Francis's love for poverty and his solicitude for the poor is something that Pope Francis yearns for the Catholic Church to emulate. The pope teaches that, for us to be able to help the poor, we must live simply and cultivate an attitude that is open to sharing. He was not pleased with bishops who spent lavish amounts on their own comforts, and he publicly reproached the so-called "bishop of bling" in Germany. Furthermore, he is often drawn to the poorest people in his midst, comforting his flock with his kisses, embraces, prayers, and reassurances. He is a good shepherd who models himself after the Good Shepherd. He is solicitous for his flock, and he desires the faithful to follow in his footsteps.

Like John Paul II and Benedict XVI, Pope Francis is an advocate for the environment. Recall that St. John Paul II declared St. Francis of Assisi the patron saint of ecology in 1979. Care for creation was an issue that always remained close to the heart of John Paul II. The same can be said of Pope Benedict XVI, who declared in *Caritas in Veritate* that human beings must respect creation and learn how to foster virtues that will enable us to live in harmony with our brothers and sisters and with all of God's creatures.

One way to recognize the importance of St. Francis for Pope Francis is the significance of the poor man from Assisi for St. Ignatius of Loyola, the founder of the Society of Jesus, which is the religious order of which Pope Francis is a member. Before his conversion, Ignatius was like Francis in many ways, attracted to battle and the goods of the world, including money, women, and parties. When a cannonball struck him in the knee, however, he was confined to a bed, where he began to read the lives of the saints. The life of St. Francis of Assisi struck Ignatius deeply, and he felt compelled to imitate him rather than to advance in the world. Through the impact of St. Francis, St. Ignatius of Loyola reformed his life and became the founder of the Society of Jesus. Today we have a Jesuit pope, who knows how important Francis was for Ignatius—and how important he is for the world—which is why he chose to be named after Francis of Assisi.

The examples of St. Francis of Assisi and of Pope Francis signify an important message to our society: the purpose of our existence is defined not by our possessions but by our relationships with God and with our brothers and sisters. For this reason, of course, detachment from material things is crucial to the

Christian life. Without detachment, people tend to close in on themselves and confine their circle of concern to themselves or a limited number of family members. Simplicity and detachment enable Christians to combat the vices of selfishness and pride, and prepare them for service to the poor, thus enabling them to follow the teachings of Jesus more closely. May the example of Pope Francis inspire Christians everywhere to live simple lives, respect the earth, and come to the assistance of the poor.

# The Importance of St. Francis for Our Time

St. Francis of Assisi is a tremendously important saint for our time. His emphasis on humility, poverty, and concern for the poor are perennial calls in keeping with the core message of Jesus; they are biblically based, radical, and prophetic. No Christian can argue against the importance the Gospels laid on being humble—that is, poor in spirit—or against Jesus' teaching that his followers were to feed the hungry, give drink to the thirsty, and clothe the naked. This call, because it stands against the spirit of the world, is also radical and prophetic. It is a calling for each Christian to repent and for Christians everywhere to become countercultural by rejecting the materialistic ideologies that media organizations and advertising agencies inject into Western society's consciousness.

Our capitalistic society emphasizes pulling oneself up by one's own bootstraps and making one's own way to the top of the economic ladder, or as high as one can possibly reach. While there is nothing inherently wrong with making a legitimate and honest living, the emphasis on individuality that pervades our society often causes people to overlook the plight of the poor or even to believe that the poor owe their impoverished state to their own purported laziness. While this may be true of some of the poor, it is not fair to make sweeping judgments that allege all of the poor to be slothful parasites who live off taxpayers' hard-earned money.

In addition to this widespread bias against the poor, our society is thoroughly materialistic. Consumerism promises happiness, as if the acquisition of novel technologies, exciting vehicles, and spacious homes were capable of satisfying all the wants of the human heart. Many people today have traded out church attendance on Sundays for shopping in malls. Name brands become patron saints, and vendors become idolized; greed is sated, and mammon is worshipped, while the poor are left to starve and die in the streets.

The joy St. Francis derived from his poverty clearly demonstrates that the spirit and promises of consumerism are but lies craftily formulated by the devil. True happiness comes from the knowledge that one is loved by God and is being faithful to the Lord of heaven and earth, to whom belong all good things. True happiness comes about through spiritual communion with family members and friends and through a clean conscience and service to the poor. True happiness comes about through detachment from material goods and attachment to God. Our society's tendency to waste is tied to consumerism. The Western world wastes a large amount of food, water, time, money, and energy that could be used to alleviate the suffering of the poor.

Francis's love of nature and his status as the patron saint of ecology shine a light on our society's lack of concern to God's creation. Today, when nature is seen as raw material to be exploited at will without regard for its future preservation or the effects its use may have on other people, it is more important than ever to bring back to life Francis's vision of a cosmos that has sprung forth from God and is bound together precisely because of this divine origin. Recognition of this dependence on divine providence is necessary if human beings are to realize that they are not the rulers of creation but merely its stewards, who have a responsibility to use nature in accordance with the laws of God. For this reason, human beings are called to discover the laws of ecological equilibrium and ought to be careful not to disrupt sensitive ecosystems. At the same time, an overemphasis on nature over and against human beings would be wrong. This is where Francis's solicitude for the poor comes into play. The poor must be given a home and must be permitted to use the resources to which they have a right.

Perhaps the most important reason why St. Francis is significant for our time is because his devotion to Jesus Christ and his call to Christians to get back to basics—by living lives of penance in accordance with the Gospel—are so fitting for our society. This spirit of Christianity is sadly missing from many Christians' lives, and the result is scandal. Francis, by contrast, was an image of Jesus Christ crucified, who in turn is the perfect image of God the Father. By following in the footsteps of St. Francis of Assisi, Christians will be better able to imitate the life of Christ and will be strengthened to take up a life dedicated to penance, prayer, and service. The world needs the spirit of Jesus; it needs the Holy Spirit; it needs the Gospel. Only by being faithful to our baptismal promises will we transform the world from within and thereby prepare God's creation for the renewal of the earth. May St. Francis inspire Christians everywhere to follow the Gospel more closely. St. Francis of Assisi, pray for us!

## References and Suggestions for Further Reading


Armstrong, Regis J. and Ignatius C. Brady, trans. *Francis and Clare: The Complete Works*. The Classics of Western Spirituality. New York/Mahwah, NJ: Paulist, 1982.

———. *True Joy: The Wisdom of Francis and Clare.* Edited by Doug Fisher. New York/Mahwah, NJ: Paulist, 1996.

Bergoglio, Jose Mario and Abraham Skorka. *On Heaven and Earth.* Translated by Alejandro Bermudez and Howard Goodman. Edited by in Spanish by Diego F. Rosemberg. New York: Image, 2010.

Bodo, Murray. *The Threefold Way of Saint Francis.* New York/Mahwah, NJ: Paulist, 2000.

*Bonaventure. The Life of St. Francis of Assisi: A Biography of Saint Francis of Assisi and Stories of His Followers. Charlotte, NC: TAN, 2010.*

———. *The Soul's Journey into God; The Tree of Life; The Life of St. Francis.* Translated by Ewert Cousins. The Classics of Western Spirituality. New York: Paulist, 1978.

*Burr, David. The Spiritual Franciscans: From Protest to Persecution in the Century After Saint Francis. University Park: The Pennsylvania State University Press, 2001.*

Chesterton, G. K. *Saint Francis of Assisi*. Peabody, MA: Hendrickson, 2008.

Clare of Assisi. *The Lady: Clare of Assisi: Early Documents*. Edited and translated by Regis J. Armstrong. New York: New City Press, 2006.

Cook, William R. *Francis of Assisi: The Way of Poverty and Humility*. Eugene, OR: Wipf & Stock, 1989.

Cowley, Patrick. *Franciscan Rise and Fall*. London: J. M. Dent & Sons, 1933.

Cunningham, Lawrence S. *Francis of Assisi: Performing the Gospel*. Grand Rapids, MI: William B. Eerdmans, 2004.

"Franciscans in the Americas." *Epic World History: Expanding the world into first global age*. http://epicworldhistory.blogspot.com/2012/06/franciscans-in-americas.html. Accessed June 9, 2014.

House, Adrian. *Francis of Assisi: A Revolutionary Life*. Mahwah, NJ: Hidden Spring, 2001.

Martin, Valerie. *Salvation: Scenes from the Life of St. Francis*. New York: Alfred A. Knopf, 2001.

Simsic, Wayne. *Living the Wisdom of St. Francis*. New York/Mahwah, NJ: Paulist, 2001.

*Talbot, John Michael and Steve Rabey. The Lessons of St. Francis: How to Bring Simplicity and Spirituality into Your Daily Life. New York: Plume, 1997.*

Talbot, John Michael. *Reflections on St. Francis*. Collegeville, MN: Liturgical Press, 2009.

*Thomas of Celano. The Francis Trilogy of Thomas of Celano: The Life of Saint Francis; The Remembrance of the Desire of Soul; The Treatise on the Miracles of Saint Francis. Edited by Regis J. Armstrong, J. A. Wayne Hellmann, William J. Short. Hyde Park, NY: New City Press, 2004.*

Thompson, Augustine. *Francis of Assisi: A New Biography*. Ithaca, NY: Cornell University Press, 2012.

# St. Teresa of Calcutta

# Introduction

In 1979, someone asked a small, elderly woman, who was dressed in a simple, perhaps odd-looking, blue and white dress, what an individual could do to promote peace in the world. The woman quickly answered: "Go home and love your family." Coming from such an individual, one might find the answer simple and even a bit naïve. However, this woman was not just any woman; she was Mother Teresa. At the time, she was the leader of a wildly successful international religious community, served as a beacon of hope for the world, and had recently been awarded the Nobel Peace Prize. Obviously, she was not naïve, and she did possess expertise on promoting peace in the world. So what could this seemingly simple response mean?

As we will see in the chapters that follow, Mother Teresa always lived a life in which she was at home and loving her family. This might seem like a strange claim since Mother Teresa constantly traveled the globe, helping the poor and needy around the world. However, this fact should not lead us to discount her claim. Rather, it should encourage us to see in her answer something more than meets the eye—something more complex than what the words might first imply.

Throughout her life, Mother Teresa worked to transform our ideas of home, love, and family. As a figure of the 20th century, she saw the rapid changes taking place in the world and among its people, and she was intuitive enough to know that Catholicism, as well as its missionary work, would need to re-imagine itself in order to meet newly emerging and diverse needs. However, she brought about transformation in a simple and unassuming way. She simply asked individuals to contemplate the meaning of ideas such as home, love, and family and to be open to new conceptions of these terms in the midst of our changing world. In doing so, Mother Teresa introduced a new, modern way of doing missionary work, led an international religious organization, and was beloved by people the world over for the work she did out of love for her family, which would one day grow to include all of humanity.

## Chapter One: Mother Teresa's Origins

In August of 1910, in the town of Skopje, in what is today the Republic of Macedonia, a tiny baby named Agnes Gonxha Bojaxhiu came into the world. She was born into an Albanian Catholic family during the calm of the earliest days of the twentieth century, in those brief moments before two World Wars would tear Europe apart, before the threat of communism would consume the West, and before decolonization movements the world over would redraw maps time and time again. This child would never grow to great heights, indeed never reaching more than a mere five feet tall; yet her image, dominated by a smile that engulfed a face of a thousand wrinkles, would be known the world over, and her deeds would distinguish her as one of the 20th century's greatest humanitarians.

It would not be long, only two years in fact, before Agnes's land was consumed by war. Her people would be ostracized and attacked, once for their ethnicity and then again for their religion. With the

Ottoman Empire crumbling in the early 1910s, the Balkans, the land immediately west of modern-day Turkey, erupted into the type of violence that can only be fueled by ethnic and religious strife centuries in the making.

Positioned not far from what was once Constantinople, the city that for much of history had been the meeting ground between West and East, the Balkans of the early 20th century was composed of a great diversity of peoples. There were a number of different ethnic groups in the region, including Serbs, Albanians, Bulgarians, Greeks, and Turks. There were a number of religious divisions as well, divisions that at times fell along ethnic lines and at other times cut straight across them. During the early Middle Ages, the region had been dominated by Orthodox Christianity as well as a sizable Jewish population. Later, some in the region, including many Albanians, converted to Catholicism. There was yet another wave of conversions, primarily amongst the Albanian people, as Islam moved into the region and later became the official religion of the Ottoman Empire.

Despite all of this turmoil, Agnes's earliest days were happy and content. She was born to Nikola (father) and Drana (mother) Bojaxhiu. She had two older siblings: a sister, Aga, and a brother, Lazar. The date of her birth is disputed, but Agnes always claimed that her "true" birthday was August 27, the day she was baptized into the Catholic Church. They were a happy family and fairly well-off. Nikola worked a number of odd jobs, and the family attended their local Catholic church. However, as the ethnic and religious strife of the region came to Skopje, Nikola became increasingly involved in city politics.

With the fall of the Ottoman Empire, the power structure that had kept the numerous differences of the region in check disappeared as well. Violence erupted not only between the different ethnic groups of the region but also amongst the different religions. During Agnes's earliest days, the Serbs, a majority of whom practiced the Orthodox faith, were able to step in and fill the political vacuum in the region. The Albanians quickly found themselves living in a land that was not their own, both ethnically and religiously. As a result, an Albanian Independence movement grew quickly in numbers and support, and Nikola became increasingly involved in its activities. This movement resulted in the creation of an Albanian state in 1912. The drawing of such national borders is, of course, always the result of arbitrary and political decisions, and thus a great number of Albanians, including those living in Skopje, found themselves living in lands not contained within these borders. What is more, the Albanian nation that was created was dominated by those of the Muslim religion, leaving Catholic Albanians torn between their nation and their faith. Families such as the Bojaxhius thus found themselves in increasingly complicated and dangerous times. As Albanians, they had, overnight, become foreigners in the Serbian-dominated lands in which they lived, yet the nation that they might have called home did not reflect their religious convictions.

These regional tensions were only heightened and exacerbated with the outbreak of World War One in

1914. The war was instigated by the assassination of Archduke Ferdinand of Austria in Sarajevo, another Balkan city only a day's travel from Skopje. Soon after, the European powers began to move into the area, further fueling the ethnic and religious differences in the region in order to use them for their own global ends.

Little is know for certain about Nikola's actions at this time. As an Albanian, was he working with factions of the independence movement that wanted to extend the national borders to include the city of Skopje as well? Or was he working with other, smaller fringe factions, which aimed to ensure the safety and freedom of the region's Catholic minority to practice its faith alongside the Orthodox Christians and Muslims who dominated regional politics? Perhaps all we may ever know for certain is that Nikola died, quite quickly and unexpectedly, in 1919, when Agnes was only eight or nine years old. There has been much speculation, but no answers, as to the cause of his death. It is widely thought, however, that he was likely poisoned by one of any number of political foes.

What must it have been like for young Agnes, growing up in such tumultuous times? One can only imagine the conversations that would have taken place around the dinner table and that might have formed her earliest memories. These might have included impassioned speeches about devotion to one's religion and people and about the will to stand up for one's identity and beliefs, even in the face of the harshest and most violent adversity. Such ideas must have been staples of Agnes's early life. However, these political teachings absorbed from her father would find new meaning as Drana, Agnes's mother, took charge of the family in the wake of Nikola's death. Drana began turning the family away from the treachery of politics and toward the safety and compassion of the Church.

# Chapter Two: Her Father's Death and the Turn Toward Religion

Nikola's death devastated the family. Not only had they lost their father; they had also lost their sole bread-winner. They quickly went from a comfortable middle-class lifestyle to one in which food was scarce and times were hard. Despite their hardships, Drana, Agnes's mother, was unwavering in her faith in God's goodness and compassion. Drana was the family's rock, and Agnes became extremely close with her. Thus, as Drana increasingly turned to the church and its teachings to sustain herself, so too did Agnes and the rest of the family.

One teaching that the family took especially seriously, and quite literally, was Jesus' command to love thy neighbor as thyself. This is most obvious from the way in which their dinners began to change. The tumultuous times in Skopje, and the region at large, had produced disastrous effects not only for the Bojaxhiu family but also for many other ordinary individuals and families. Skopje began to fill up with destitute people—victims of the catastrophic violence in the region who had lost their homes, families, and livelihoods. Drana, in the face of such desperate need, threw open the doors of her house and began to invite the hungry and needy to join her family at their dinner table. Indeed, it seemed that no matter how scarce the family's food reserves became, Drana was always able to add another dinner plate to the table. She refused to let others go hungry if her family was able to eat. As we will see, this was a lesson Agnes would carry with her throughout her life: whatever one had was never so scarce that it could not be divided and shared with another in need. As Drana told the young Agnes, "My child, never eat a single mouthful unless you are sharing it with others."

For a long time, Agnes assumed that the individuals who joined her family at dinner were friends from town or church. However, upon asking her mother once about those who joined them at their table, Drana responded, "Some of them are our relations, but all of them are our people." How different the dinners at the Bojaxhiu household had become! When her father was alive and the family was directly embroiled in the political events of Skopje and the region at large, meals were most likely filled with conversations about political tensions and oppositions outlining "us" versus "them": Serbs versus Albanians; Christians versus Muslims; Catholics versus Orthodox. Now, these lines and concerns began to blur into the background as any hungry person, whether Albanian or Serb, Orthodox or Catholic, was welcome in their home and at their table.

In fact, her commitment to others led Agnes to learn the Serbian-Croatian language, and she began serving as a translator for individuals at the family's church and in other situations. The distinctions that so divided the region continued to disintegrate for her as she began to form deep connections with members of groups other than her own. In short, the family's turn toward religion, initiated by her mother in response to her father's death, was creating a shift in whom Agnes understood to be her "people"—that is, to which individuals she felt connected and of which groups she felt herself to be a part. In place of political, ethnic, and religious divisions, Agnes was beginning to see everyone as members of one community, united through Christ's sacrifice and in God's love.

However, it was not by means of these dinners alone that the family put their Catholic faith into practice. In the summers, they joined their church on a month-long pilgrimage to the shrine of Our Lady of Cernagore, located in what is today Letnica, Kosovo. These pilgrimages took the family into the mountains north of the city and were a happy relief for Agnes. Skopje is located at the base of a valley, with the Vardar River running right through its city center. The climate is fairly warm and humid, and this took a toll on the sickly Agnes, who suffered through both malaria and whooping cough as a child. For Agnes, these pilgrimages were not only spiritually fulfilling but also a healthy retreat to a more temperate and agreeable climate.

There is little doubt that these pilgrimages were a formative time for Agnes's relationship with God. They healed her body and also served her soul, giving her time to reflect and contemplate, which came naturally to the serious, introverted child. These reflections prompted the development of the highly personal connection she felt with God, the depths of which the world would come to know only after her death.

Drana's lessons about God's love and Jesus' commandment to love one's neighbor, whatever their religion and ethnicity might be, would be fundamental to Agnes's future actions and achievements. Indeed, Agnes would take these beliefs and further expand upon them until the whole world would truly become her people. This, however, does not mean that Agnes did not gain anything from her father's more political sensibilities, for the world in which Agnes was growing up in and in which she would become an actor of global consequence was rapidly changing. The political lessons Agnes learned from her father would serve her many times throughout her life as she brought love for God and neighbor to the world's poor and those afflicted by colonialism and the decolonization movements, cold wars, cultural wars, and many other 20th-century affairs.

# Chapter Three: Mother Teresa's First Religious Calling

Drana's strength and commitment to the church, as well as the family's yearly visits to a shrine devoted to the Virgin Mother, taught Agnes yet another important lesson. In the Virgin, as well as in her mother, she saw the enormous potential that women of faith had and the impact that they could have on the world. Through these two figures, Agnes learned that she did not need to sit on the sidelines; the power of God flowed through her, and she could have an overwhelmingly positive effect on "her people."

It was on one of her family's summer pilgrimages, in 1922, that Agnes first felt called to a religious life. She was twelve at the time, and it was then that she knew she would devote her life to doing God's work. At the time, she was not exactly sure what this meant, but she put her faith in God and threw herself into church activities.

It was for this reason that she began to learn about the long history of Catholic missionary work, including missions to the land today known as India. She loved hearing stories about the exotic lands and the difficult but fulfilling work of the missionaries. She began to dream of going on such adventures herself. However, in the 1920s, missionary work was done almost exclusively by men. What was a young girl with hopes and dreams like those of Agnes to do?

Luckily, a priest at her church introduced her to an Irish order of nuns known as the Loreto Sisters of Dublin. The order was founded in the 17th century and had, from its inception, been doing pioneering work. Since the 17th century, the nuns had journeyed throughout the world, serving as teachers to the local children of whatever land they found themselves in. They even had schools in India, the land that most excited Agnes's interest and compassion. In 1841, twelve nuns from the Sisters of Loreto had traveled to the Indian city of Calcutta in order to establish a school there. Their success in India grew quickly. By 1842, they had 60 students at their school, called Loreto House, and within three years they had expanded to three boarding schools and three days schools and had established two orphanages as well.

Here was the opportunity for which Agnes had been praying! Here was a group of women who—like Mary, the Virgin mother, as well as her own mother—did not sit back passively; they took an active role in bringing God's word to the world. What is more, they did so in the very land that so ignited Agnes's imagination. Finally, Agnes understood the meaning of the calling that she had first felt at only twelve years of age. In 1928, Agnes decided to join the Loreto Sisters of Dublin and become a nun.

We must not think that this was an easy decision for the young Agnes. Far from it. After much prayer and introspection, she was certain that this was what God had called her to do. However, devoting herself to God and becoming a nun for an Irish order, with the hope of one day teaching in India, would mean leaving her family, her church, and the land in which she had grown up, all of which she loved fiercely. Perhaps even more significantly, it would mean leaving her mother, her rock, with the possibility that she might never see her again. Indeed, Agnes agonized over her decision, as did her mother.

However, Drana, who as her daughter's role model understood Agnes's devotion to God so well, was the one who, in the end, insisted that this was what Agnes must do with the rest of her life.

And so, at the tender age of 18, Agnes packed up the few possessions she would need, left everyone and everything she had ever known, and journeyed to a new and foreign land. She did not go to India immediately. Rather, she traveled to Dublin, where the main branch of the Sisters of Loreto was located. It was here that Agnes would spend her postulancy, the time period (lasting anywhere from six months to a year) during which an individual lives with the order she plans to join, takes part in their daily activities, and prays to God to determine whether she has, in fact, correctly understood her calling and has made the right decision in choosing to become a nun.

In addition to praying, Agnes also spent a lot of time learning more about the history of the order and their teaching exploits around the world, and she practiced the English language. This was the primary language of the order and also the language in which she would be expected to teach in India. Agnes, of course, missed her mother and the rest of her family terribly. However, by the end of 1928, she was certain that she had made the right choice in devoting her life to the work of God and was excited to set off on new adventures.

In another way, Agnes's decision to join the Sisters of Loreto and leave her homeland in search of foreign adventures was a pragmatic and fortuitous one. The end of the First World War in November of 1918 had left the Balkans in ruins. What stability had arisen in the region during the 1910s after the fall of the Ottomans, if any, was wiped away by the onslaught of global politics and occupation by European powers. What is more, the League of Nations, an international body founded after World War One and meant to maintain world peace by determining ethnic and territorial disputes, began imposing new and arbitrary political boundaries in the region. Again ethnicities and religions were divided by national borders, and in response, massive deportations and relocations were initiated throughout the region. The war, as well as the later population movements, devastated the region socially and economically.

In short, Agnes confronted a dire situation in her homeland. What possible future was there for her if she remained in Skopje? In many ways, perhaps it was better for her to leave her homeland and make a new start. True, the land to which she would journey, and which she would ultimately call her new home and country, was itself on the verge of monumental and often violent change, but there was also the potential to do God's work there and serve her fellow man. With that intention, Agnes bravely set out into the world.

# Chapter Four: Voyage to India

On December 1, 1928, with her postulancy at an end, Agnes boarded a boat with a fellow friend and nun and set off for India. Five weeks later, after a long and arduous voyage at sea, she arrived in Darjeeling, on January 5, 1929. Finally, she was in the land of which she had dreamed for so long. It was here that she would spend her novitiate period, lasting a total of two years. The novitiate period is a time between a future nun's postulancy and her taking of vows. In this time period, both the future nun and her order have agreed that she has been called to a life of service and devotion to God. The novitiate is thus the period during which a woman learns all that will be expected of her once she takes her vows and becomes a nun. For Agnes, this meant her continued study of English in preparation for her teaching duties. She also began to study both the Bengali and Hindi languages so that, when the time came, she would be better able to serve the people around her.

The land that had once been a mere figment of her wildest dreams quickly became a reality for the young Agnes. In some ways she found herself in a land rather similar to the homeland she had left behind, but in other ways the country and its culture were markedly different. Agnes had much to learn.

Like the Balkans, India is a land afflicted by ancient ethnic and religious differences that have erupted into violence at numerous times throughout the centuries. It is home to many different groups of people as well as many different religions. The majority of Indians practice Hinduism; however, beginning in the 12th century, a sizable Muslim minority began to develop. Since the 15th century, there has been a substantial number of Sikhs, practitioners of a monotheistic religion that originated in the northwestern region of India. India is also home to many Christians. Missionary work in India had been occurring for centuries before groups such as the Sisters of Loreto arrived to the land in the 19th century. In fact, the first Catholic missionaries were from Portugal and came as early as the 1500s, at the beginning of European voyage and expansion around the globe.

Missionary presence in India, including the schools started and maintained by the Sisters of Loreto, did increase considerably in the 1800s, thanks in large part to British colonial rule. For centuries, India had been the spice capital of the world, and the economic and political ties between India and Europe—and Britain in particular—were long and deep. The East India Company, an English trade organization, was first formed in 1600 and took exclusive trading rights over all business involving Indian goods and resources. Due to the company's financial success in the region, the land became an official colony of the British Empire in 1612. By the 1800s, the British Empire was at its height; it was a tightly-knit, well-oiled machine that spanned the globe. This impressive organization made possible the type of social work that missionaries carried out.

However, by the early 1900s, Britain's empire was crumbling. Its sway over its lands was rapidly dwindling, due in large part to toll that the First World War had taken on England. Confronted by real and immediate dangers at home, English was unable to continue to support and control its far-flung colonies around the globe. By the end of the 1920s, India was a land on the verge of massive change and upheaval. In 1930, just a year after Agnes's arrival in India, a disobedience movement advocating nonviolent methods such as hunger strikes arose, led by the famed Mahatma Gandhi. This movement called for an end to British colonial rule and the beginning of Indian self-governance. Yet again, Agnes found herself in a land where people were divided and political power and borders were unstable and fraught.

In addition to this political unrest, Agnes also confronted a social system unlike anything she had experience in her homeland or in her short time in Dublin. The caste system in India has a long and complicated history, made even more complex by the British government's exploitation of the system in order to maintain peace in the country during colonial times. What can be said for certain is that, by the time Agnes arrived in India, the caste system was a deep-seated and powerful social organization that had an impact on the minds and daily realities of the

Indian people. According to the caste system, people were divided into groups, including Brahmins, Kshatriyas, Vaishyas, and Shudras. Each group served a different role in society. Brahmins were known as the priestly caste, Kshatriayas were the warriors, Vaishyas were merchants and landowners, and Shudras were the servant class. Group membership was inherited according to birth, and divisions between the groups, even those involving such basic social interactions as interactions in a shop or a nod on the street, were strictly maintained. Each group also possessed differing amounts of social, political, and economic capital, and as a result, they were organized hierarchically, with some groups having much more power than others.

One group in particular, the Dalits, was excluded from this hierarchy completely. Also known as "untouchables," members of this group were thought to have no role and were essentially excluded from taking part in society in any way. They did not—indeed, due to the rigidity of the divisions imposed by the caste system, could not—have direct interactions with members of any of the castes; and if they were even able to find work, they only did the most menial of labor. As a result, they were poor and downtrodden and had little ability or support within Indian society to improve their situation. This also meant that, as tensions rose in India with the growth of the disobedience movement and waning of British control, this group was disproportionately affected by the negative impact that these tensions had on the Indian population. Disease and hunger were rampant, and because of the social stigma barring interaction between these people and members of other castes, there was little in the way of medical care or social services. In almost all ways, these people had been forgotten, left to suffer and die alone.

In time, these very people, the untouchables of India, would become Agnes's people. That, however, was still years in the future, after Agnes had already lived what many would find to be a full and successful life as a nun and teacher.

On May 24, 1931, Agnes took yet another monumental step in this direction, undertaking her First Profession of Vows and becoming a full member of the Sisters of Loreto. It was at this time that she took the name by which the world would come to remember her by: Teresa. She chose the name in honor of Saint Thérèse of Lisieux. Saint Thérèse, known by many as "The Little Flower," was a French Carmelite nun who died tragically of tuberculosis in 1897 at the young age of 24. Although she had spent much of her short life secluded from the world in a convent, her writings about her deep and personal relationship with God have become known the world over. She was also famous for her devotion to, and prays for priests, especially those conducting missionary work. Upon her canonization, in 1925, she was deemed the patron saint of missionaries.

There is little doubt why Agnes chose the namesake she did. Like Saint Thérèse, she too had participated in a deep and spiritual relationship with God from a young age; and like Saint Thérèse, she was also captivated by the work being done by missionaries.

However, unlike her namesake, Agnes would not be content to remain in her convent. Instead, she would go out into the world to meet with, and advocate for, the poor and needy, all the while radically reshaping the way in which missionary work was done.

# Chapter Five: Mother Teresa's Teaching Years

Upon becoming a nun, Agnes, now known as Sister Teresa, moved to Calcutta to begin her teaching career. By this time, the Sisters of Loreto had become well-established in Calcutta, known for their superior ability to teach local children English, a highly necessary skill if one were to be successful in Indian society. By the 1930s, the order had established a compound of sorts in Calcutta—a large set of walls that separated their many schools from the city at large. They had a total of 500 students, with a majority coming from wealthy families who were able to pay the tuition necessary to fund and maintain the schools. The nuns left the shelter of the compound walls rarely, if ever. This meant that, given the socioeconomic status of most of their students, they were often unaware of many of the hardships taking place amongst the lowest and most destitute of India's population.

Sister Teresa's situation was a bit different. She began teaching geography and history at Saint Mary's, a school housed within the compound. Unlike many of the other schools, however, Saint Mary's catered to an economically and socially mixed group of students from a variety of backgrounds. What is more, many of the teachers alongside whom she worked were not missionaries who had come to India but, rather, Christian women from India. Many of them had been educated by the Sisters of Loreto and later become nuns themselves. These women did not wear the traditional nun's habit, as Sister Teresa and the other missionary teachers did at the time, but rather wore saris, or traditional Indian dresses.

In this way, Sister Teresa became aware of aspects of Indian society that were unknown to many of her fellow nuns. Her students and fellow teachers offered her intimate accounts documenting the issues faced by many of the lower classes due to the rigid social system in place in India, issues that were only exacerbated by the politics of the time. It was in this way that Sister Teresa was first introduced to the plight of people living right outside the walls of the compound that she called home. The poor and untouchables of Calcutta who were her neighbors now.

She became even more starkly aware of the urgency of their situation when, in 1935, she was given a special exemption to teach at the school of Saint Teresa. The school was located beyond the walls of her order's compound, and this meant that Sister Teresa had to go on daily walks through the city of Calcutta as she commuted to and from the school. It was during the course of these walks that she encountered firsthand what her students and fellow teachers at Saint Mary's could only describe to her. The people's plight was worse than anything she could have imagined, even though she had heard many stories. She encountered poor and unfortunate people everywhere, living alone and starving in dirty, makeshift slums. Many had simply been left to die in the streets, often for no other reason than their lack of social status.

One cannot help but wonder whether, in addition to provoking her love and compassion for the poorest of India, this experience might not also have left Sister Teresa feeling a bit frustrated. She had left everyone and everything she had known and loved behind in order to go off into the world and serve God's people, and certainly, as a Sister of Loreto and a teacher at Saint Mary's, she was doing precisely that. And yet, a mere 10 feet from her classroom, on the other side of a dividing wall, people—her neighbors—were dying in the streets. She could not have helped but notice that within the walls of her compound, by and large, were found those of higher social and economic standing in India while those outside of its walls were the people most negatively affected by such social divisions—those made "untouchable" by the caste system. Sister Teresa had already seen the unnecessary and overwhelmingly negative effects that these types of arbitrary social divisions had caused in her homeland. Indeed, her short life had been filled with the kind of violence to which these types of divisions so often give way. However, thanks to the lessons she had learned from her mother and the family dinners they used to have back in Skopje, Sister Teresa would not be persuaded by, or content with, such divisions. She devoutly knew that all people were her people; all people were one in God.

There was surely some way in which she could serve those who most needed her. However, in 1935, such thoughts would only have been in their infancy for Sister Teresa. It would be many years yet before she was able to put them fully into action.

Until that time, Sister Teresa would continue to teach within the compound at Saint Mary's. On May 24, 1937, she took her Final Profession of Vows, fully committing herself to the life of poverty, chastity, and obedience expected of a nun of the Sisters of Loreto. It was at this time that she took on the title of "Mother," giving her the name we all hold so dearly today: Mother Teresa. She was a hard and diligent teacher. She expected much of her students but also showed them endless love. Over the years, she affected many devoted young girls who would later, as women, become her followers.

In 1944, 15 years after she first began to teach in India, Mother Teresa became the principal of Saint Mary's. She was 34 years old, and in many ways she had already achieved everything for which she had hoped and prayed as a little girl while on summer pilgrimages with her family in the mountains north of Skopje. She had become a Sister of Loreto, she had moved to India as a Catholic missionary, and she served the people by teaching their children. Despite all of her success, she would not remain content for long. She could not forget the plight of those people who lived beyond the walls of the compound; they may have been forgotten by the rest of the world, but Mother Teresa would remember them, and she would act.

# Chapter Six: Mother Teresa's Second Religious Calling

In 1943, a horrific famine swept across the region. Its causes were numerous. There had been crop failures several years in a row as well as a terrible and destructive cyclone. In addition, the region's resources had been increasingly depleted by the onslaught of World War Two. At home, India was also afflicted by crippling government corruption. In 1935, Britain had passed the Government of India Act. While India remained a British colony, the act granted it a large amount of autonomy. Unfortunately, the young government was not yet stable enough to address such a crisis successfully, and a number of inept policy failures stopped food reserves from reaching the people. Millions perished.

As the principal of her school, Mother Teresa was responsible for her students and her teachers alike. On several occasions during these difficult times, she had to leave the confines of the compound walls in order to search for food. This was an eye-opening experience for her. If her school was suffering from the famine, this suffering was incomparable to that of the city's poor and untouchables who lived beyond the walls of her compound.

The lack of resources, as well as government wrongdoing, increased tensions amongst the different peoples of India. Most notably, violence began breaking out between the land's Hindu and Muslim populations. Tensions were especially high in Calcutta, a city of millions, the population of which was split between Muslims and Hindus. On August 16, 1946, tensions boiled over in Calcutta. Known today as the "Great Calcutta Killings," riots between Muslims and Hindus erupted throughout the city. Three days later, 4,000 people had been killed, and over 100,000 people had been left homeless.

Mother Teresa just happened to choose August 16, of all days, to go out into the city in search of food for her school. What she saw shocked her. There were people killing each other in the streets while amongst the bodies lay the poor and starving. Calcutta was a city coming apart at the seams. Although teaching children at Saint Mary's was a noble task, surely there was something she could do to address the pain and suffering that surrounded her school. There must be something more she could do for India; there must be something more she could do for her neighbors—for her people.

On September 10, 1946, less than a month after this horrific event, Mother Teresa and the rest of her order left Calcutta by train for their annual retreat in the Himalayan foothills. While they were on this train ride, Christ came to Mother Teresa and spoke to her. He told her that he no longer wanted her to teach; he wanted her to leave the confines of her school to go into the slums and work with the poorest and sickest of India. Later, Mother Teresa would call this day her "Day of Inspiration," the day that God called her for a second time.

Although today this idea might seem commonplace—the idea, that is, to live and work with the people who are the most in need—we ought not overlook how unprecedented Mother Teresa's plan was at the time. As we will remember, missionary work in India, including the work done by the Sisters of Loreto, was made possible in large part by the colonial structures put in place by the British government. Inevitably then, these missions came to reflect the structures that supported them. For example, the colonial system benefited from the maintenance of the caste system because it offered the British government a way to order and control the population. This meant that the British government did not actively address the plight of the untouchables of India, those individuals excluded from the caste system entirely and barred from basic contact with the rest of society.

Similarly, missionaries in India had done much to help the people of India. However, they too did not directly serve the poorest and most needy of India. Instead, as the Sisters of Loreto did, they served India's middle classes. This is not to say that the middle classes of India did not desire or benefit from the word of God; they certainly did. Unfortunately, the social system in place at the time made it such that, by serving those groups, missionaries ended up not serving—or, in the case of the Sisters of Loreto, literally building walls to separate themselves from—the most needy in Indian society. The missionary system that had arisen during the colonial period certainly served some of the people of India, but it did not address the plight of the poor who lived in the slums at the outskirts of society.

Mother Teresa's calling challenged this way of doing missionary work. Indeed, in a world that was quickly changing as postcolonial movements around the globe gained ground in the wake of World War Two and redrew borders, she would offer a radically new way of doing missionary work. In short, she would introduce a modern way of bringing God's word to the people of the world, and in doing so she would propel Catholic missionary work into the 20th century.

Despite God's command, however, accomplishing this feat was no simple task. As a Sister of Loreto, Mother Teresa had taken a vow of obedience to the order. She could not simply pick up her belongings and leave them. Instead, she would have to get special permission from the Vatican to grant her leave from her duties with the Sisters. Thus, Mother Teresa launched a campaign, writing letters to the pope and lobbying her local archbishop; she begged them to allow her to fulfill God's plan for her.

In January of 1948, a year and a half after Christ had come to her, she received approval from His Grace Ferdinand Périer, archbishop of Calcutta, to pursue her new calling. He gave her a year to prove that her plan for a new, modern way of doing missionary work could be successful. He asked her to keep a diary, documenting not only her successes and failures in the community but also her own personal struggles and achievements. Mother Teresa would go on to keep a diary for much of the rest of her life, and its contents, including her documentation of her deep and sometimes complicated relationship with God, would be revealed to the world only after her death.

In August of 1948, her life as a teacher already fulfilled, 38-year-old Mother Teresa left the Loreto convent that she had called home for the last 20 years. Yet again, she was leaving behind everything and everyone she knew and setting off into the world in order to do God's work. She did not, however, enter the slums and immediately begin working with the people. Instead, she left Calcutta and went to stay with a different order of nuns in India, known as the Medical Mission Sisters. She thereby learned the basic nursing skills that were so desperately needed, yet so lacking, amongst the poor and untouchable classes. After six months, she went back to Calcutta and entered the slums.

# Chapter Seven: The Origins of the Sisters of Charity

After spending several months training with the Medical Mission Sisters, Mother Teresa returned to the city of Calcutta in December of 1948. But what exactly was she to do for the poor now that she had finally received this opportunity? She would have to be innovative and creative because there was no model for her to follow. The people whom she wanted to help were the very people forgotten by the established colonial systems, whether those systems be governmental or religious.

The first change that she made was to live with the people whom she intended to serve. She did not construct a wall around herself or divide herself from the people she so desperately wanted to serve, as had been the case with the compound of schools operated by the Sisters of Loreto; rather, she moved into the slums with the people. She ate, slept, and passed her days with them. For Mother Teresa, there would never again be a division, physical or otherwise, between her and other people—between her and her neighbors. In this way, she was putting into action the lesson she had learned so long ago around her family's dinner table back in Skopje: just as her mother had invited anyone and everyone who was hungry into their house, so too did Mother Teresa make her home with those most in need. As her mother had taught her, they may not be her relations, but they were "her people."

In order to demonstrate her connection to the poor of India, Mother Teresa even went so far as to change the way she dressed. She decided that she would no longer wear the traditional black and white habit donned by the Sisters of Loreto; instead, she chose to dress in the simple blue and white sari for which she would later become famous. In fact, her dress was similar to the Indian women with whom she had worked at Saint Mary's for so many years. Moreover, its simplicity ensured that she met the poor as their equal, down to the very fabric she wore.

But what would she do besides live as an equal with these people? Obviously, she had a little medical training, thanks to the time she had spent with the Medical Mission Sisters; however, she was no expert in this area. She was, though, an expert in teaching, so she began to teach the children of the slums. She could not simply open up a school since she had no capital. Instead, she began by writing in the dirt with a stick and teaching the children out in the open air. As time went on, she was able to find her own living quarters in the area. She also found a hut, which she could rent at the extremely low rate of five rupees per month, and this served as her first schoolhouse.

In March of 1949, she received a special visitor. Subhasini Das was a former pupil of Mother Teresa's from Saint Mary's, and she had heard of the important work that Mother Teresa had been doing for the poor. She had come to join Mother Teresa and help her with her labors. Subhasini became Mother Teresa's first helper and remained her devoted aid throughout her lifetime. Subhasini was quickly followed by 10 other women. Many were former students like Subhasini, and several others had been teachers alongside Mother Teresa at Saint Mary's. All had been inspired by her—by her commitment to God and her drive to connect with and help the poor of India.

This was an extremely significant moment for Mother Teresa. Most importantly, she was no longer a single individual acting upon Jesus' calling; now she was the leader of a small but growing religious community that was the embodiment of this calling. Her growing community was also a tangible mark of her success. Practically speaking, this was crucial if she was to fulfill the archbishop's command to prove herself within a year. This success ensured that she and her vision would retain the support of the Church.

1949 was a significant year for Mother Teresa in another way as well, for it was in this year that she applied for and received her Indian citizenship. In doing so, she had completely re-envisioned who she saw as her "people," thanks in large part to the lessons of her mother. It had not been enough to live with, dress like, and work amongst the poor; now she shared her national allegiance with them as well. How far she had come from her early beginnings and her father's involvement in the fight for the rights of Catholic Albanians. She had crossed oceans and traveled to new lands, and now she found herself united not only with people of a different ethnicity than her own but also many people who did not even share her religion. But such were no longer Mother Teresa's concerns, for now, as a servant of God, she was doing Jesus' will by serving those most in need, no matter their earthly allegiances. She knew that, in God's eyes, they were all His children and, therefore, they were all her neighbors; she was merely doing His will by serving them.

This is not to say that the political lessons she had learned from her father were not useful to her at this time. Indeed, far from it. India had gained its independence from Britain on August 15, 1947. At the same time that the country was shedding the trappings of colonial rule and re-imagining itself as the world's most populous democracy, so too was Mother Teresa re-imagining missionary work in a world after colonialism. The political timeliness of her actions should not be overlooked. By the late 1940s, India was ripe for change, both politically and socially, and Mother Teresa was wise enough to make the most of this moment. By transforming the way in which missionary work was performed, she was ensuring that the Catholic Church would be able to adapt its message to a changing world. This type of transformation could only be achieved by an extremely intelligent and politically aware mind.

On October 7, 1950, Mother Teresa officially received the acknowledgment that she had sought upon leaving the walls of the Sisters of Loreto. On this day, Pope Pius XII bestowed canonical recognition on her growing religious community. Now her group of Catholic women, primarily Indian women who had first met her as teachers and students during her days at Saint Mary's, became known as the congregation of the "Missionaries of Charity" in the Archdiocese of Calcutta. Their official mission was to "serve the suffering Christ, whom they saw in the poorest of the poor."

# Chapter Eight: The Early Days of the Sisters of Charity

Mother Teresa and the newly recognized Sisters of Charity did not take their mission lightly. She demanded that they lead a very regimented day. They awoke early in the morning, took a short lunch, and went to bed long after dark. Much of their day was devoted to direct interaction with the poor, teaching and caring for them. A portion of every day was also set aside for prayer and contemplation. If the sisters served Christ by serving the poor, then they needed to cultivate and develop their relationship with God in order to ground their work in His love.

Their numbers quickly grew, and as they did, so too did the number of people they were able to serve. Using her political acumen, Mother Teresa began to take advantage of a law recently passed by the new government. This law stated that, for every 100 children, the government was required to build and maintain a school building. The more women who joined her ranks, the more teachers she was able to train; and the more teachers she had, the more children her sisters were able to serve. In this way, Mother Teresa was able to have several school buildings built without spending any of her own money.

Thanks to the good work her sisters were doing, she began to come to the attention of Indian officials. Independence had not been easy for the young nation. The country continued to be rocked by the same ethnic and religious violence that had so impacted Mother Teresa during her time with the Sisters of Loreto. In fact, just a month after gaining its independence from Great Britain, these tensions literally tore the country apart as the land was partitioned into India and Pakistan. This was followed by widespread violence and bloodshed, resulting in the deaths of hundreds of thousands of people. India was further shaken by the assassination of Mahatma Gandhi in 1948, followed by a war with Pakistan over the disputed territory of Kashmir. In short, the young government was so consumed by political troubles that it had little time or energy to focus on its own citizens, especially the poorest and most destitute. Mother Teresa and the Sisters of Charity filled this void, and the government was thankful for and supportive of all of the important work they were doing.

For this reason, several Indian officials came to Mother Teresa's aide in her first attempts to branch out from education. They helped her to locate and fund the conversion of a deserted Hindu temple into her first home for the dying. Ever since her first trip beyond the walls of the Sisters' of Loreto compound, Mother Teresa had been distraught by the numbers of individuals she had encountered who were, quite literally, left to die alone in the streets. Most, if not all, of these individuals were member of the untouchable class, and it was therefore taboo for any individual of a different caste to interact with them. As a result, those individuals who were best able to help and support these individuals—doctors, nurses, social workers and so on—did not do so and, at least according to social convention, were unable to do so. Mother Teresa, as well as the Indian officials who supported her, hoped that her home for the dying would fill this void and offer solace to these poor souls in their hour of need. The home opened on

August 22, 1952, and was called Kalighat or Nirmal Hriday, which in English means "Place of the Immaculate Heart."

She and the Sisters of Charity branched out yet again in 1955. By this time they had developed a firmly established network of schools for the children who lived in the slums of Calcutta. However, many of these same children were living on the streets, and a great number of them had been orphaned, whether because of rampant disease and lack of healthcare in these areas or because of the pervasive violence that continued to afflict the country. Mother Teresa realized that it was not enough simply to teach these children; she and her sisters needed to give them a home. For this reason, the Sisters of Charity opened up their first orphanage, which they called Nirmala Shishu Bhavan, or the Children's Home of the Immaculate Heart. This home was only the first of many, and by 1958 the sisters had facilities for 90 children.

Around this same time, Mother Teresa also realized that not only was the caste system barring many of Calcutta's poorest from obtaining health services but so too was their inability, whether because of illness or due to lack of resources, to travel to such services. She therefore organized her first mobile clinic in 1956. The vehicle was outfitted with all of the needs of a medical clinic and traveled throughout Calcutta's slums, seeking out individuals in need of care.

These early homes and services were essential for the later development of the Sisters of Charity, for through them, Mother Teresa was able to establish her general approach to caring for those in need and her new, modern approach to missionary work. In all of her endeavors, she offered individuals both support for their most pressing material needs—whether access to education or healthcare or a safe and comforting place to live and die—and spiritual rejuvenation and salvation. Through Mother Teresa's work, many of India's poor were introduced to Jesus Christ for the first time. In short, Mother Teresa cared for and supported individuals in their needs for this life as well as the next.

Mother Teresa's approach was also influenced by the dinners that her mother used to host back in Skopje. Just as her mother had always found a way to share their meager food rations with any and all who joined their family at the dinner table, so too did Mother Teresa ensure that she and the Sisters of Charity shared all of their wealth and solace with as many people as possible. This meant that her orphanages, clinics, and homes often offered only modest accommodations. However, as her mother had taught her so many years before, there was never so little that it could not be divided and shared with others. Mother Teresa took this lesson to heart and was always concerned with the number of individuals she was able to support.

This was an essential part of the way in which Mother Teresa was beginning to re-imagine Catholic missionary work in the changing world of the late 1940s and 1950s. In the wake of postcolonial movements around the globe, as with the events taking place in India, vast numbers of poor individuals who had been excluded and oppressed by the recently ousted colonial system were now emerging from the hidden margins of society. The numbers of people in need of help skyrocketed. Mother Teresa realized that missionary work would have to vastly re-conceptualize the sheer numbers of people whom these projects would be able to serve in the coming years, and she enacted the lessons of her mother in order to do so.

Around this time, Mother Teresa's work began to come to the attention of the Indian press, and several articles were written about her good deeds. These articles earned her many devoted admirers, and those with the means began to donate to the Sisters of Charity. Mother Teresa immediately used these increased funds to open more homes and clinics. Her impact on the poor of India was beginning to increase rapidly.

According to canon law, a new order such as the Missionaries of Charity could not open up a second mission until 10 years after its original founding. This rule, of course, was meant to ensure the success of the original mission, barring it from stretching itself and its resources too thin, too soon. Mother Teresa, made impatient by this rule given her immense success, began making plans to expand to other Indian cities, and she opened several missions a few months before the 10-year deadline. In 1963, with the opening of the Missionary Brothers of Charity, the Missionaries of Charity officially expanded to include men as well.

In 1960, Mother Teresa embarked upon yet another new and previously unthinkable project. Today many of us may think of leprosy as a thing of the past, even perhaps of the Biblical past. However, this was not the case in India during the middle of the twentieth century. In fact, on the outskirts of many cities, including Calcutta, makeshift colonies of lepers had sprung up, and as many as 30,000 individuals afflicted with the disease lived in India alone. These colonies were places of disease and suffering, avoided by most out of fear of contamination. Placing her trust in God, however, Mother Teresa went into these colonies without fear for herself, intent upon easing the suffering of those living there. She even opened up a home for lepers, known as Shanti Nagar or Place of Peace.

In addition to the ways in which Mother Teresa was transforming missionary work, there are two other important conclusions to be drawn from these early, developmental days of the Missionaries of Charity. The first is Mother Teresa's organizational and political skill and dexterity. In only a few years and with little money, she was able to create a vast network of homes and clinics that served the diverse needs of India's poorest communities. Furthermore, she did so in such a way that she was able to capitalize upon the domestic political void in India, which was a consequence of its government's international concerns and laws. The second lesson is Mother Teresa's ever-expanding understanding of who composed "her people" and of who she would consider to be her neighbors. With the expansion not simply into the slums of India but also into the country's leper colonies, Mother Teresa was showing the world that all people—whether tabooed, diseased, or both—no matter what society thought of them, were her people. She truly understood the claim that all people are God's children and, thus, all people were her neighbors. With this in mind, she organized the Missionaries of Charity so that they fully embodied and acted upon this principle.

# Chapter Nine: Mother Teresa's First Trip Abroad

Mother Teresa's success, as well as the new approach to missionary work that she was developing, had caught the eye not only of the Indian press but also of people outside the borders of India. Catholics around the globe increasingly began to talk about the little woman in India, in the simple blue and white sari, who was doing so much good for the poor and destitute. Many people, especially many Catholic women, began looking upon her as a role model. It was for this reason that Mother Teresa was invited to visit the United States in 1960 and speak at the annual meeting of the National Council for Catholic Women in Las Vegas, Nevada.

This would be the first time in 30 years that Mother Teresa would step foot outside the borders of her adopted homeland of India. She traveled to Las Vegas and gave her speech. Mother Teresa spoke frankly and simply to her audience, in what would become known as her characteristic style. She spoke of her devotion to God. She spoke about her conviction that one served Jesus when one served the poorest of the poor. Speaking of her compassion for God's people, she challenged her audience to re-imagine who those people were and whom they might consider to be their neighbors. Just as her mother had taught her that God did not see ethnic divisions such as Albanian or Serbian, Mother Teresa now taught her audience that God did not see divisions such as rich or poor, Western or Eastern, Catholic or Hindu. All of humanity was God's people, and thus a commitment to God meant a commitment to help the poorest and most destitute of humanity, whoever and wherever they might be. She spoke straight from the heart and without notes. Although many had known of her before this time, this speech certainly thrust her into the spotlight for Catholics in America.

From Nevada, she continued her tour of the United States, stopping in both Illinois and New York. Her time in New York left a lasting impression on her as she found the city to be in need of exactly the type of work that she and the Missionaries of Charity did. A little more than 10 years later, she would have the opportunity to act upon this belief.

She decided to take this opportunity to travel to Europe as well before returning to India. She went to London, Germany, and Switzerland and was met by throngs of supporters at every stop. She also stopped in Rome, where her brother had taken up residence after fleeing their war-torn and devastated homeland in the Balkans. Mother Teresa had not see Lazar in over 30 years, and their lives had taken very different paths. Lazar had joined the Albanian army as a young man. During World War Two, Albania was occupied by Italy, and Lazar had joined the Italian army and become a fervent support of its fascist regime. Despite their differences, they were overjoyed to see one another. They even attempted to devise a plan to have Mother Teresa visit her mother and sister, who had remained in the Balkans and were living in Albania. Unfortunately, after World War Two, Albania had become a ruthless communist regime, tightly controlled by its government. There was no way for Drana and Aga to leave Albania and no way for Mother Teresa, quickly becoming a Western celebrity and thus a potential enemy of the Albanian state, to enter the country. Sadly, this is as close as Mother Teresa would ever come to seeing her mother again.

While in Rome, she was granted an audience with the pope at the time, John XXIII. What a monumental moment this must have been for Mother Teresa. She had been a devoted Catholic for such a long time and had committed her life to serving Jesus, and the opportunity to meet the leader of her religion must have been overwhelming, to say the least. Nevertheless, always keenly aware of the opportunities presented to her, she used the occasion to ask the pope to consider granting her the decree that would allow the Missionaries of Charity to expand internationally. Here we find yet more evidence of Mother Teresa's exceptional political sensibility, inherited from her father, and a prime example of the way she used this gift to do the will of God and serve her people—that is, the people of the world.

By 1960, the year of this tour, Mother Teresa was 50 years old, and in many ways she had already had the successes of two lifetimes. For almost 20 years, she had been a beloved teacher and principal. Then she had become the founder of an extremely successful new religious order in India that was reshaping Catholic missionary work. For many people, this would have been more than enough; they would have been satisfied with their life's work. Not so for Mother Teresa. She used this trip as the opportunity to open up yet another chapter of her life and find another means by which she might serve the living Christ and cater to the poorest of the poor.

However, it was not only the pope's decree that she and her sisters would need if they wanted to begin working internationally. They would also need money, for such an endeavor would be incredibly expensive. Again, Mother Teresa's political know-how came into use. As she traveled around the world, she met Catholics throughout the United States and Europe. She told them of her work in India and of her hopes and dreams for the future. Her ideas inspired many of her listeners, and they quickly recognized that Mother Teresa was a woman of her word. If she said that she wanted to create a successful group of international missions, then she would do it. They also recognized that they could provide the capital to help her make this possible. Many people began donating to the Missionaries of Charity, producing the funds necessary for the next stage in Mother Teresa's service to God. Indeed, the publicity and connections that she was able to generate during this trip would, in many ways, be just as important as her audience with the pope had been.

# Chapter Ten: The Sisters of Charity Go International

During her audience with Pope John XXIII, Mother Teresa had asked him for the *decretum laudis,* or decree of praise. Receiving the decree of praise is extremely significant for a religious community such as the Missionaries of Charity. The decree of praise recognizes the success and maturity of a congregation and makes it subject no longer to a diocese but to the Holy See itself. It was this type of recognition that would grant Mother Teresa permission to expand the Sisters of Charity beyond India to become an international mission. Five years later, in 1965, Pope Paul VI granted her this decree.

Mother Teresa wasted little time. She decided to follow the same pattern of growth that had already proven so successful in India. The sisters would go to a new location and open up a house from which to serve the poorest and most destitute of the land—those who, like the untouchables of India, had been brushed aside and forgotten by their fellow citizens and neighbors. Once the house had been established, the sisters would begin to develop schools, orphanages, homes for the dying, and leper colonies, if applicable. Continuing to follow the lessons she had learned from the dinners her mother hosted so many years earlier, Mother Teresa would make the most of the money she had at hand. While ensuring that the mission provided adequate care to those who came there for help, they would always find ways to stretch their pennies so that they were able to serve all who were in need of their love and attention. They would also continue to wear the blue and white sari, as Mother Teresa had first donned years earlier, making them instantaneously recognizable throughout the world.

When determining where she would open her first house, Mother Teresa turned to an Australian archbishop and future cardinal named James Knox. Knox had been serving in India for 10 years and had seen first-hand the impressive work and successes that Mother Teresa's tenacity had made possible. He had become one of her strongest supporters and advocates. Therefore, when he heard of the growing need in Venezuela, he recommended Mother Teresa as the perfect person to take up the challenge. In July of 1965, Mother Teresa and the Sisters of Charity opened up their first mission outside of India, a home in Cocorote, Venezuela.

The Venezuelan venture was wildly successful, and it affirmed Mother Teresa's plan to follow the pattern laid out in India. Building on their success, the Sisters quickly expanded. In 1967, they opened a home in Sri Lanka. This was followed, in 1968, by homes in Tanzania, Austria, and the slums of Rome. In 1971, she even fulfilled the dream ignited by her trip to America a decade earlier and opened up a home in New York City. In every case, the Sisters of Charity went to parts of the world that had populations in need and who were not being served by their fellow citizens and neighbors; in short, they went where they were most needed and could do the most good.

In 1969, she was awarded the Jawaharlal Nehru Award for International Understanding. The Indian government awards the prize yearly to one individual, of any nationality, whom they find has made an "outstanding contribution to the promotion of international understanding, goodwill and friendship among people of the world." True, it was only the first of many awards to come for Mother Teresa; however, this award, given at the time that it was, is perhaps particularly symbolic. For one thing, it seems quite fitting that she be recognized by her adopted country. The award recognized the work that she had been doing not only in India but also throughout the world. In this way, the award serves as a tangible marker of the monumental transition taking place in her life. It is almost as if, by awarding her an international award, India was recognizing that she was no longer theirs alone; they realized that, now and in the future, they would be sharing her with all peoples and nations.

This award also serves as a testament to Mother Teresa's ever-evolving understanding of who "her people" were. She had begun life with a quite narrow definition, recognizing her connection only with other Catholic Albanians. Under the influence of her mother, she had challenged this understanding as a young girl and started to see her connection with those of other ethnicities and religions who lived around her. She had then moved to India, recognizing her connection not only to those of her home region but also to those of her newly adopted land. Yet again, she began to challenge this understanding by moving into the slums and living with those individuals deemed untouchable by traditional Indian society. Now no one could deny that even the least of the least were her people and her neighbors. She had gone to the people who most needed her and given herself to them, and in turn they saw and accepted her as one of their own. She further solidified this transformation by expanding her missions internationally. It was not only the poorest of the poor in India with whom she identified herself but the poorest of the world as well, wherever they might be.

The step to take the Sisters of Charity international ensured the lasting success of the revolutionary changes that Mother Teresa was making to missionary work during the 20th century. She showed the world that all people everywhere, no matter how sick or destitute, no matter how forgotten or ignored by their fellow citizens and neighbors, were God's children and that, for this reason, they were her people as well. Mother Teresa had seen first-hand a number of turbulent events that pointed to the radical ways in which the world was changing. First, in her homeland, she saw the increasingly violent tensions between ethnic groups and the faltering of European stability. Then, in India, she witnessed the violent effects of decolonization. Mother Teresa, ever politically aware, knew that the world was fundamentally shifting and, if missionary work was going to continue to do God's will and serve the living Christ, then it would have to transform, too. More specifically, missionary practices that had developed during, and found support in, colonial expansion would have to be radically rethought. Missionaries could no longer maintain a separation from those they served, for this was increasingly seen as maintaining outdated colonial habits and, furthermore, often overlooked those who had been excluded from those systems and left most in need. Now, thanks to Mother Teresa, missionaries would go to the people and become one with them. Mother

Teresa’s rapid international growth pointed overwhelmingly to the success of this new approach.

# Chapter Eleven: The Muggeridge Interview, Film, and Book

While Mother Teresa's first international trip in 1960 revealed her growing celebrity amongst the world's Catholics, one event in particular is credited with skyrocketing her to fame throughout the whole of the Western world. In 1968, she agreed to do an interview for the BBC with a then-renowned reporter named Malcolm Muggeridge. Immediately, a number of her closest aides and supports were against the idea, begging her to rescind the offer. Muggeridge had made a name for himself by loudly and publicly stating his own atheistic beliefs as well as his opposition to all forms of religion. He was also known for being an abrasive interviewer who enjoyed taking oppositional and negative positions in his work. Mother Teresa's supporters feared that he would conduct an unfair interview and would attempt to discredit the "little woman from India" and attempt to make a mockery of her.

Mother Teresa, however, was unmoved by such concerns and calmly asserted that she would go on with the interview. Here was a woman who had put her full faith in God. She knew that she had been called by Jesus to do the work she was doing; what care did she have for the way in which other might attempt to present it? It was a risk, nonetheless, but a risk worth taking. Never losing sight of the political and organizational needs of her (now international) religious community, this interview, if successful, would be exactly the type of publicity that the Sisters of Charity needed. The more the world heard of their good deeds, the more missions and services they would be able to open and maintain.

Thus, Muggeridge and Mother Teresa met in London to conduct the interview. To the surprise of all involved—well, all save Mother Teresa, perhaps—the two got along splendidly, and the interview was a great success. The BBC replayed it multiple times to an ever-growing audience. Mother Teresa, of course, had made it her life's work to show the world that all people were her people; she had connected with the poor around the world, so why not add a brash British atheist to the list as well? Muggeridge had apparently gone into the interview expecting Mother Teresa to be proud, overbearing, and judgmental.

Instead, he found himself in conversation with a woman who spoke in simple and unassuming terms about the incredible work that she was doing. Her primary and overwhelming concern was always the love she felt for the poorest of the poor and her drive to help them in any way she could. She had little time to worry about people such as Muggeridge and even less time to judge them. God's people were her people, and this included Muggeridge, whatever his views might be.

Muggeridge was greatly moved by Mother Teresa's simple yet profound message of love. He found himself thinking repeatedly about the things she had said to him during their interview. As a result, Muggeridge entered into a crisis of faith, if one can apply such a term to a dedicated atheist. He even began to explore the Christianity that he had condemned for so long. In 1969, he began practicing the faith and wrote a book about his experience, entitled *Jesus Rediscovered.*

The interview had not only affected Muggeridge but had impacted his BBC viewers as well. Funds began pouring in to the Sisters of Charity, despite the fact that Mother Teresa never asked for money during the interview. Instead, people simply understood the great work that she was doing and wanted to find some way to support her. Clearly, Mother Teresa's new approach to missionary work was speaking to people. As the Sisters continued to grow internationally, this type of publicity and support would become an increasingly important component of their work.

In the same year as his conversion, Muggeridge decided to visit Mother Teresa in India. His plan was to make a documentary film about her work. Incredibly, they shot the film in only five days and did not encounter any of the typical equipment failures or other obstacles that so often plague on-location shootings in an exotic place. If this were not miracle enough, Muggeridge himself claims to have encountered a miracle when they were shooting at one of the Sisters' many homes for the dying.

According to Muggeridge, his cameraman did not think it would be possible to shoot in the dark space. Muggeridge, however, thought that it was essential to introduce the world to all of Mother Teresa's work, perhaps most especially the way she cared for those so close to death without fear or judgment. Then, almost as if on cue, according to Muggeridge's account, the room was filled with a warm and bright light, making it possible for them to film inside the building.

The film was called *Something Beautiful for God* and met with almost instantaneous international support. Muggeridge followed up the film two year later with a book about Mother Teresa, also called *Something Beautiful for God,* which has now been translated into at least 13 languages. The title of the film comes from a letter that Mother Teresa wrote to Muggeridge shortly after his visit to India. In it she tells Muggeridge that he should, in his own way, "try to make the world conscious that it is never too late to do something beautiful for God." According to many, it was the film and book that launched Mother Teresa into international fame. With these two pieces, people around the world, whether Catholic or not, were introduced to the daunting work to which she had committed her life.

Let us pause to consider the words of Mother Teresa that became the inspiration for this film and movie. They were, of course, meant for Muggeridge and most likely were addressing his late-in-life turn toward Christianity. However, they could have been referring just as readily to Mother Teresa's own life. As we have seen, Mother Teresa was never satisfied with her work; she was always searching for ways in which she might continue to serve God. It was this drive that compelled her to leave Saint Mary's after almost 20 years as a successful teacher and principal, and it was the same drive that led her to look beyond the borders of India and to concern herself with the world's poor. Not only was it never too late to do something beautiful for God but it was also never too late to do something *more* beautiful for God. In this quote, we find Mother Teresa teaching us always to be on the lookout for new ways to serve God, whether by actions we had not previously considered or by serving poor and destitute individuals of whom we had not previously been aware. In these words, Mother Teresa challenges us always to remain open and to be prepared to encounter God, perhaps often where we least expect to find Him.

The film brought the Sisters of Charity international fame, and it served an important role in the new missionary framework that Mother Teresa had developed. One of the most notable changes Mother Teresa had introduced to missionary work in the 20th century was her directive to go to the people one was serving and become one with them. For Mother Teresa, as she had seen so many times in her life, it was essential that individuals tear down the ethnic, religious, and social borders that divided them from one another. In some ways, the film and book were a means of doing just that. For many in the West, it was easy to remain unaware of poverty in the world, such as the situation of untouchables in India. These were people whom Westerners did not encounter on a daily basis. In fact, given the way in which many

Western cities developed, many Westerners did not even interact with the poor and destitute in their own communities. This film, then, served as a wake-up call for many. Not only did it introduce Westerners to the plight of people in India but it also offered them a role model. Mother Teresa was only a little woman in a simple blue and white sari who had devoted her life to loving these individuals and improving their lives. If she could do such a thing, then others too could begin to address the poverty and suffering of their neighbors. Moreover, the film and book prompted many Westerners to think about how they defined "their people," in the same way that Mother Teresa was always looking to expand the definition of who "her people" were: Whom were they going to love, and to whom were they going to commit themselves to helping in the hour of need?

While a huge number of Westerners took up this call by offering financial support to the Sisters of Charity and their many projects around the world, some went even further. In 1970, the Sisters of Charity received 139 new candidates. Unlike in previous years, this year's group of candidates consisted of individuals from all over the world. These were individuals who had learned of Mother Teresa's good work and had heeded her call that, to serve God, one must love those most in need and become one with them through service, no matter who they are or where they might be.

By 1975, thanks to the incredible increase in donations initiated by Mother Teresa's ever-growing prominence and popularity, the Sisters of Charity had been able to open 32 homes for the dying, 67 colonies for lepers, and 28 children's homes in locations around the world. What could Mother Teresa hope to achieve next?

# Chapter Twelve: The Nobel Peace Prize and Other Awards

What followed for Mother Teresa, besides the continuing development of the Sisters' of Charity work around the world, was a number of significant awards.

In 1971, she was awarded the first Pope John XXIII Peace Prize by Pope Paul VI. The award was not to be given annually; rather it was developed to be given only to an exceptional individual who was doing exceptional work to promote peace in the world. By selecting Mother Teresa as its first recipient, Paul VI was setting the bar high. Indeed, the award has only been given out a handful of times since. This must have been an especially significant award for Mother Teresa, as the religion to which she had devoted her life returned her devotion by acknowledging the importance of her life's innovative work. Furthermore, her labors were revolutionizing the way in which Catholic missionaries approached the world and the way in which the world perceived this work. Mother Teresa was an incredibly positive influence in the world for Catholicism, and the Church recognized this and made its appreciation known.

In 1979, at the age of 69, she was awarded the Nobel Peace Prize. In fact, this was not the first year she had been nominated; she had been nominated but passed over for the award three previous times. One of the strongest advocates for her nomination and selection for the award was Robert McNamara, who was a former American Defense secretary and the director of the World Bank at the time. In Mother Teresa's work, he found levels of success in serving the poor that were unthinkable in the organization where he worked, and he greatly admired her for this. He had worked for a number of years to have her awarded the Nobel.

Upon learning of her selection for the award, Mother Teresa told reporters in India, "I accept the prize in the name of the poor ... The prize is the recognition of the poor world ... By serving the poor I am serving Him." She went to Oslo to accept the prize. She asked that the extravagant banquet traditionally held in honor of the recipient be canceled and requested that all expenses be donated to the poor. She did decide to give a speech in front of the Hague, as was customary. As she had many years ago in Las Vegas in front of the National Council for Catholic Women, and again in her interview with Muggeridge, she spoke simply and from the heart. Speaking of love, that seemingly simple yet profound commandment, she explained: "It is not enough for us to say: I love God, but I do not love my neighbor. St. John says you are a liar if you say you love God and you don't love your neighbor. How can you love God whom you do not see, if you do not love your neighbor whom you see, whom you touch, with whom you live? … We have been created in his image. We have been created to love and be loved, and then he has become man to make it possible for us to love as he loved us. He makes himself the hungry one—the naked one—the homeless one—the sick one—the one in prison—the lonely one—the unwanted one—and he says: You did it to me." In this quotation, Mother Teresa reveals to us the constant struggle that we must face if we are to love as Jesus commands us. For it is in those very moments when we least feel like loving someone—when we want to turn away from, blame, or ignore him or her—that she challenges us to see God in this individual and to love that person. Every time we find ourselves confronting another who is different from us in some way, whether by location, religion, ethnicity, or social status, we must work to see beyond and tear down those divisions, recognizing that other people are our neighbors—that we are all one and we are all God's people.

In 1980, she was awarded the Bharat Ratna, or Jewel of India, award. It is the highest honor that can be bestowed on an Indian civilian, and Mother Teresa is the only naturalized citizen to have ever won. Much like the Jawaharlal Nehru Award awarded her in 1969, this particular award must have had special significance for Mother Teresa. However, whereas the Jawaharlal Nehru recognized her work both in India and abroad, the Jewel of India went one step further and acknowledged that this work was done by an Indian citizen worthy of honor. It must have seemed like ages, maybe even lifetimes, ago that she had left the Sisters of Loreto and decided to become an Indian citizen. Now, all of these years later, the country of which she had dreamed, and which she had accepted as her own, reciprocated this love, recognizing her as not merely one of their own but also as one of their most upstanding citizens.

In 1985, Mother Teresa was given the honor of addressing the United Nations General Assembly on the occasion of its 40th anniversary. When introducing her, Secretary General Pérez de Cuélliar said what many around the world felt: "I don't think I need to present her. She doesn't need words. She does need deeds. I think that the best thing I can do is to pay tribute to her and to tell that she is much more than I, much more than all of us. She is the United Nations. She is peace in this world."

It was not only the West that recognized the significant impact Mother Teresa was making on the world. In 1987, the USSR honored her by bestowing upon her the Gold Medal of the Soviet Peace Committee. Obviously, in 1987, an individual would have to be quite exceptional for both the West and the USSR to honor him or her. But of course, it is perhaps not surprising that Mother Teresa was such as person.

# Chapter Thirteen: Mother Teresa and the Crisis in Beirut

In 1982, war broke out between Israel and Lebanon. The years leading up to the war had been a tumultuous time for the Middle East. Lebanon in particular had felt the effects of these times as it had been entrenched in an overt civil war since 1975. The war erupted, at least in part, because of the unleashing of ethnic and religious tensions as the Middle East went through its own process of decolonization. In Lebanon alone, there was fighting between Sunni and Shiite Muslim factions, Christians, as well as ethnic Palestinians. The Palestinian Liberation Organization had become increasingly organized and militarized. This, in turn, raised the suspicions of Israel, Lebanon's neighbor to the south. With its own sizable minority population of Palestinians, Israel was heavily invested in and concerned by the PLO's activities and, thus, the fighting in Lebanon in general.

The tensions between Israel and Lebanon came to a head on June 3, 1982, when the Israeli Ambassador Shlomo Argov was shot and seriously wounded in London. The attack was attributed to the Abu Nidal terrorist organization, the headquarters of which were in Lebanon. The Israelis used the attack as justification for launching an offensive into southern Lebanon, where the Palestinian Liberation Organization was taking refuge. Only seven days later, the Israelis had surrounded Beirut, Lebanon's capital city. For the next seven weeks, they attacked the city by air, ground, and sea in what has become known as the Siege of Beirut. With intentions of ending the fighting quickly and decisively, the Israeli offensive was intense and brutal in order to overwhelm Beirut swiftly.

Into the middle of all of this chaos and violence stepped Mother Teresa. She had been asked by Pope John Paul II to act as his personal emissary during the conflict. The Pope's selection of Mother Teresa for this role was strategic for a number of reasons. Firstly, she was by this time recognized worldwide as a symbol of peace. If the Catholic Church wanted to express its hope that the violence be stopped and the conflict ended, who better to bring this message than Mother Teresa? Furthermore, Mother Teresa was loved and respected around the world, not only by Catholics but also by people of all races, creeds, and walks of life. For this reason, her presence ensured neutrality on the part of the Catholic Church.

However, we ought not discount the importance of Mother Teresa's historical background and political acumen. Although the actors and tensions were different than those in the Balkans, Mother Teresa was intimately aware of the way in which religious and ethnic opposition can rip a region apart. She also had experience, beginning with those dinners her mother had hosted so long ago, of dissolving these differences in order to unite people. Finally, Mother Teresa was the leader of an overwhelmingly successful international religious order. She clearly understood how to deal with the inevitable politics that would arise in such a situation, and she would be able to transfer this knowledge to her activities in the Middle East.

She arrived in Lebanon on August 11th, a month into the siege. She was closely followed by a huge throng of media. Everyone wanted to know what the "little lady from India" could do in the face of something as seemingly intractable as Middle Eastern politics. The media's attention made it difficult for her to do much covertly, but two days later she was nevertheless able to slip past the crowds and sneak into a part of Beirut that was seeing the worst of the fighting. She was going to visit what she thought was an Islamic home for the dying that many believed had been hit by Israeli artillery. However, when she reached the hospital, what she found was not the sick and elderly but, rather, 37 scared and injured children, refugees who had been left behind and were trapped in the hospital.

Mother Teresa quickly decided that she had to save these children; however, the fighting was so intense that no one knew how she would be able to accomplish this goal without getting herself killed. But of course, the "little lady from India" was not to be underestimated, including in her political tenacity. Speaking with both sides in the conflict, Mother Teresa was able to broker a momentary cease-fire that provided her and the children with safe passage to a Red Cross camp, which was located away from the fighting. Mother Teresa took the children there, where her Sisters could go about caring for them.

Can we imagine any other individual in the world capable of accomplishing such a feat? Rare is the person who is able to bring two warring factions to the table in order to broker a peace deal; even rarer is the individual who is able to do so in the Middle East. Mother Teresa truly was a phenomenal individual touched by God.

This incident was also exemplary of the extent to which Mother Teresa believed that love could reach. As she had said at the UN, it was not enough to love God abstractly; one must show this love by caring for one's neighbor. And who were Mother Teresa's neighbors? As we have seen, her understanding of who "her people" were had continually evolved. However, by 1982, as an international figure and Nobel Prize Winner, it was clear that the whole world was Mother Teresa's neighbor. If individuals were in danger or pain, Mother Teresa too felt this pain and was compelled to do something to ameliorate it, even if that meant risking her own life by walking into an active war zone and standing up to world powers. Indeed, Mother Teresa's love knew no bounds.

Mother Teresa was 72 years old at the time of the Lebanon War; however, despite her age, this conflict marked the transition into yet another phase of her life. Before the conflict, Mother Teresa's international actions had revolved primarily around opening missions and securing support and backing for those missions. Now, however, as the Beirut Crisis had shown, Mother Teresa was discovering that her presence alone could be a significant step in resolving conflicts and addressing the plight of the poorest of the poor around the world. In the years to come, Mother Teresa would use this ability—the ability to insert herself into situations—in order to create peace, time and time again.

# Chapter Fourteen: Mother Teresa's Involvement in Other Global Crises

There are three world events of particular note during this period of Mother Teresa's life: the disaster in Bhopal, the Ethiopian famine, and the nuclear leak at Chernobyl. In every case, Mother Teresa inserted herself into the situation, using her physical presence to bring international attention to the devastation and thereby bring peace and aid to the suffering.

On the evening of December 2, 1984, in Bhopal, India, there was a horrible chemical gas leak at a pesticide factory owned by Union Carbide India Limited. The disaster spewed poisonous gases into the air, which were then carried by the winds throughout the region. Estimates suggest that over 500,000 people were affected by the leak. The immediate death toll that night was 2,259. Other estimates suggest that, within weeks, as many as 16,000 people had died from complications caused by exposure to the gas. Many more were maimed months and years later by diseases brought on by the chemicals. The region was left contaminated, and its population was devastated. To make things worse, neither the company nor the Indian government acted swiftly to contain the leak or to set up services for the victims. The suffering was massive. However, the West had heard little of the events in Bhopal, and thus no entities outside of the government or company were stepping in to help the victims, either.

Mother Teresa changed all of this. Hearing of the suffering in Bhopal, she quickly decided to go on a visit to the region, in order to bring comfort to the maimed and dying. Given her international celebrity, the world was of course interested to see what the purpose of Mother Teresa's latest trip was. This was when the situation in Bhopal was revealed to many. Shortly after her trip, funding and aide began to pour into the region.

The following year, in 1985, a devastating famine was in full swing in Ethiopia. It was brought on for a variety of reasons, including decolonization followed by years of wars; a massive, extended drought; and government corruption that wasted money on military concerns rather than feeding its citizens. The world, however, paid little heed to the situation in the region, even as the death toll skyrocketed. Indeed, the UN puts the number of deaths caused by the famine as high as one million. Again, upon hearing of the situation in the region, Mother Teresa decided to travel there in order to visit with and comfort the people, and again the word took notice of her activities. Her presence in Ethiopia was both a reality check and a challenge. It was a reality check insofar as it forced many in the West to consider events in a region of the world whose people were all too often ignored by larger global powers. It was a challenge insofar as Mother Teresa's presence demanded that the world see the people of Ethiopia as their neighbors, recognizing in their suffering the suffering of Christ.

Then, on April 26, 1986, near Pripyat, Ukraine, there were complications in reactor number four of the Chernobyl Nuclear Power Plant. The situation quickly escalated, and a huge fire broke out throughout the plant. The fire, in turn, emitted a massive plume of radioactive material that affected areas of the globe stretching from Europe to Russia. Thirty-one people died in the immediate aftermath of the event, many of them emergency personnel working to contain the fallout. However, the numbers of those who have developed cancer and other health issues attributable to radiation poisoning is expected to reach into the thousands as time goes on. Furthermore, there has been a spike in the number of birth defects in regions most impacted by the fallout. With the Cold War still in full swing at the time of the disaster, the Iron Curtain separating the USSR from the West meant that the West was unable to obtain much information about the disaster. They had no idea exactly how devastating the event had been and how far the contamination stretched. Mother Teresa decided to travel to the region upon hearing about the event. The role her presence played in this event is a bit different from that in the two other events just discussed, for in this instance her presence did not simply bring to light an event about which much of the world knew nothing. Her presence, rather, also opened up communications between two world superpowers amidst a decades-long standoff.

If one were simply to look at Mother Teresa's travels in the 1980s with little regard for her history and political sensibilities, one might be surprised at her seemingly uncanny ability to show up in extremely significant places during extremely significant events. However, we know that the story is much more complicated than this. While Mother Teresa's travels certainly were compelled by God and her desire to love her neighbor to the fullest extent possible, including by traveling to areas afflicted by war, natural disaster, or chemical threat, we might also see another side to them as well. One might argue that Mother Teresa had never really lost the political tenacity on which her father had taught her to rely. This was obvious throughout Mother Teresa's life, beginning with the way in which she was able to navigate the Indian government in order to find funding for her first schools.

However, these three events and her other travels during this time period perhaps most starkly point toward the depths of her political talent. Unlike her father, she never used her political sensibilities to create oppositions or to capitalize upon them. Rather, she astutely used her presence to intervene in highly polarized situations in order to offer the neutral and universal message of love of neighbor. In every case, Mother Teresa must have been aware that she was putting herself at risk by traveling to these dangerous locations; however, she calculated that this risk was worth it if it would shed light on a situation and challenge the world to re-imagine who their neighbor was so that they might love others all the more. If she could force the world's hand by intervening in these situations through her mere presence, then how could she value her own life more highly? How better could she serve God?

# Chapter Fifteen: Mother Teresa and the AIDS Crisis—the "New Leprosy" of the West

There is one other significant crisis of the 1980s with which Mother Teresa became involved and of which it is important to take note. It again exemplifies the extent to which Mother Teresa asked us to love our neighbors. In addition, however, it demonstrates the way in which Mother Teresa was always open to the changing world around her. As new crises and forms of suffering emerged, she was always ready to confront them with an open mind in order to determine how best to serve the people who most needed her help.

New York City had bothered Mother Teresa since she had visited it on her first international trip so long ago. She simply could not fathom how the richest and most powerful nation in the world could also have the slums and destitution that existed in New York. This was perhaps especially the case with New York in the 1980s. How was it possible that those more fortunate were not helping their neighbors, their fellow citizens, in their hour of need?

When the AIDS crisis came to New York City in the 1980s, it decimated certain populations, especially homosexual men and illicit drug users. On first thought, it might seem strange to think that Mother Teresa felt compelled to take up of the cause of these individuals. However, on second thought, it is perfectly understandable, for both of these populations were pushed to the edges of society. They were often ignored and, thus, had to suffer alone without recourse to aid or resources. In so many ways, they were like the untouchables of India, with whom she had first begun to work so long ago.

In fact, Mother Teresa made this connection publicly when she announced that she believed AIDS was quickly becoming the "new leprosy" of the West. The connection is, indeed, uncanny. Like lepers, people un-afflicted by the disease were often scared to interact with the victims in any way. People refused to hug and kiss suffering family members, and many people were left to die alone in isolated hospital rooms.

The initial response to the AIDS crisis, as is well known, was to blame the individuals who had become infected by it and to judge them for their "risky" behavior. Mother Teresa was unmotivated by such arguments. Who was she to judge a person in pain? Who was she to judge another's suffering? For her, love was greater than any of these arguments. She knew that no matter what these individuals had done, they were still God's children, they were still her neighbors, and she loved them; and to love them meant to join with them in order to determine how she might serve them.

She opened up a hospice in Greenwich Village, where her sisters cared for individuals who were suffering from the disease and had nowhere else to turn. Her compassion for those afflicted with AIDS and her refusal to judge them for their actions even led her to call for and gain the release of three young men from Sing Sing Prison. All three men were suffering from advanced cases of the illness, and Mother Teresa was adamant that even they, these men who had chosen to break the laws of the land, should not have to die alone, locked away in a cell. Even they deserved to be loved and cared for in their hour of need. She had them transferred to the hospice, where her sisters cared for them until their deaths.

But what exactly is noteworthy in Mother Teresa's response to the AIDS crisis in America? Surely it was not the first disease she had decided to combat, nor was it somehow more significant than the other issues upon which she chose to focus. However, unlike other diseases, AIDS was a newly emerging disease in the early 1980s and one about which the world knew little at the time. It carried with it a social stigma perhaps not even found with leprosy, which was stigmatized but also, at least, understood by many. None of this influenced Mother Teresa; she refused to judge anyone, for any reason, no matter how contemporary or popular such prejudices might be. Again, we find the extent to which Mother Teresa was willing to love others and what it meant for her to love Jesus and to love her neighbor. It also demonstrates the way in which she constantly challenged herself to push the limits of this love. In a moment when it would have been so easy to follow social convention and look the other way and find a different disease to address, she instead challenged herself to find Christ in the pain and suffering of these individuals and to seek out how she might serve them.

Mother Teresa's response to the AIDS crisis in America also serves as yet another example of the way in which the political sensibilities she learned from her father helped her to carry out her mission to its fullest. Unlike her father, she did not use her skills and knowledge to draw divisions between individuals. Instead, as this particular example indicates, she used her knowledge to anticipate the development of such divisions. In calling AIDS the "new leprosy" of the West, she was attempting to warn the world. She was attempting to show people that, yet again, they were threatening to turn a blind eye to their fellow man and to the newest embodiment of the suffering Christ, who most needed their love and affection.

Mother Teresa was a woman ahead of her time. She was always aware of the changing social situation, whether that be the political system in India as it transitioned from colonial rule to democracy or the response to AIDS in the 1980s, and she used her political awareness to act upon these developments. This is yet another change that Mother Teresa introduced to missionary work in the 20th century. Missionaries could no longer assume that they knew who most needed their services. Rather, in a world of political and social upheaval, one had to constantly remain vigilant and open-minded as world events continuously produced new and often unanticipated victims.

# Chapter Sixteen: The Teachings of Mother Teresa and the Sisters of Charity

In 1976, the contemplative branch of the Sisters of Charity was established. But what were the teachings of this particular religious community? Like many other orders of nuns, the Sisters of Charity took vows of chastity, poverty, and obedience. Their possessions were kept to a minimum. No matter where they served in the world, they were issued only three of the blue and white saris, with the intention that they would then have one to wear, one to wash, and one to mend. They were given only two or three cotton habits as well as a girdle and pair of sandals. Of course, they also always carried a crucifix and rosary with them, as well as a prayer book, and they kept all of their belongings in a simple canvas bag. If they happened to live in a part of the world with a colder climate, they were also allowed to have a sweater and even a coat, scarf, and warm shoes. However, all of these items were only kept out of necessity.

The Sisters of Charity also adhered to a fourth vow: to give "wholehearted free service to the poorest of the poor." Mother Teresa's life, of course, serves as the ultimate example of this vow. Her teachings and speeches also help us to understand that "wholehearted" service to the poor means constantly challenging oneself to see one's neighbor in the poor and afflicted around us. This is especially important when one feels an aversion to such thinking. Whether this aversion arises from ignorance—one is simply unaware of the suffering around oneself and throughout the world—or from social and political stigma, it does not matter. Mother Teresa and the Sisters of Charity worked vigilantly to overcoming such divisions, making this challenge their life's labor. It was only by undergoing this strenuous and self-reflective work that, Mother Teresa believed, one could truly enact love in the world, understand what it meant to love God, and love one's neighbor as oneself.

Although there were many different parts to the Missionaries of Charity, Mother Teresa used the image of the five wounds of Jesus to describe their connection to one another. The two wounds in Jesus' hands represented the sisters and brothers of the Missionaries of Charity who took action throughout the world and carried out God's will. The two wounds in Jesus' feet represented the contemplative sisters and brothers. These individuals went in search of their souls and served as the spiritual counterparts to their active brothers and sisters. The wound in Jesus' heart represented the priests who served the Missionaries of Charity, supporting and nurturing their work. The body of Christ itself represented the world's poor, in desperate need of the love and care that the Missionaries of Charity were able to provide. It was love of this sacrificed body, the recognition of the suffering Christ in the suffering of those in the world, that united the world and made people one with each other.

The teachings of Mother Teresa can also be found in two of her favorite prayers. The first was written by Pope Paul VI:

> Make us worthy, Lord,
> to serve our fellow men
> throughout the world who live and die
> in poverty and hunger.

Give them through our hands,
this day their daily bread,
and by our understanding love,
give peace and joy.
Amen.

By repeating just these few phrases to himself or herself, an individual is able to recall the most significant aspects of the work done by the Missionaries of Charity. They saw the whole world as their neighbors and their fellow men, and they traveled around the world to serve them. Through their work, they aimed to bring relief to the afflicted and peace to the world.

The second prayer is a prayer by Saint Francis of Assisi, and it speaks not only to the actions of the Missionaries of Charity (as the previous prayer does) but also to the challenge that ought to guide these actions. It reads:

Lord, make me a channel of your peace, that
where there is hatred, I may bring love;

where there is wrong, I may bring the spirit of
forgiveness;
where there is discord, I may bring harmony;
where there is error, I may bring truth;
where there is doubt, I may bring faith;
where there is despair, I may bring hope;
where there are shadows, I may bring light;
where there is sadness, I may bring joy.
Lord, grant that I may seek rather
to comfort than to be comforted;
to understand than to be understood;
to love than to be loved;
for it is by forgetting self that one finds;
it is by forgiving that one is forgiven;
it is by dying that one awakens to eternal life.
Amen.

In short, the teachings of the Missionaries of Charity were grounded in a development and modernization of that simple lesson Mother Teresa learned from her mother when she was only a little girl: love thy neighbor as thyself. However, Mother Teresa showed the world that, in the rapidly changing times of the

20th century, this simple phrase was more complex than it might at first seem. For the 20th century was a world that saw two world wars, ethnic and political strife the world over, the emergence of new diseases, and natural and human-made disasters on a scale unthinkable in previous time-periods. In such a world, one's "neighbor" was no longer a simple concept. Rather, one had to challenge oneself to remain open to the changing times, constantly aware that one's neighbors might be the individuals one least expected. This meant that the act of loving one's neighbor became more complex. In order to ensure this love, one had to tear down the boundaries between oneself and others. Mother Teresa did this throughout her life, but she first did so when she decided to leave the confines of the Sisters of Loreto and live in the slums of Calcutta. To love, a person had to become one with those different from him or her; they had to recognize that all men, no matter their deeds or afflictions, were God's children and part of "their people."

One also had to consider the way in which one went about this love. It was not enough merely to say that one loved God or that one loved those who were different. Rather, one had to demonstrate this love through actions. Love meant recognizing the pain of others and attempting to ameliorate it, and it meant challenging oneself to do so in situations where one might be least likely or most unwilling to do so. Perhaps the most important teaching with which Mother Teresa left us is never to take this principle—to love thy neighbor as thyself—lightly or for granted, but rather to find in it the struggle necessary to create peace in the world.

# Chapter Seventeen: Mother Teresa's Legacy and Beatification

In 1989, Mother Teresa finally began to slow down as she suffered a severe heart attack and her health began to decline. In 1990, she informed the pope that she wanted to resign as the leader of the Missionaries of Charity. However, they quickly realized that there was no one who could take her place. It was not simply that no one else could serve as a figure of hope and beacon of peace in the way that Mother Teresa did. Indeed, it would have been unfair to expect such things from any other individual. However, they also could not find anyone with the political acumen and organizational intelligence necessary to carry out the job that Mother Teresa did. And so, as we have seen numerous times now throughout her life, she thought little of herself and her own deteriorating body and continued to work and serve her people.

By 1997, the work had finally become too much. On March 13, 1997, Mother Teresa stepped down as the leader of the Missionaries of Charity. She was succeeded by Sister Nirmala Joshi. Sister Nirmala's parents were from Nepal, and she had grown up in British India. She was raised Hindu but converted to

Catholicism after being educated in Christian schools. She had a background in political science and legal studies and had also started the contemplative branch of the Missionaries of Charity. In Sister Nirmala, Mother Teresa finally found someone who could fill her shoes. Sister Nirmala had the political smarts necessary to run a worldwide organization, but she also had the religious background and conviction to ensure that this political work was always carried out in the name of love of God and the suffering Christ.

On September 5, 1997, Mother Teresa died from heart, lung, and kidney problems. She was 87 years old. She died in peace in Calcutta, India, her adopted homeland. The government of India issued a state funeral for her, and thousands of Indians—thousands of her people—lined the streets to say goodbye to the little lady who had brought peace to the world. She is buried at the Mother House of the Missionaries of Charity in Calcutta, the place where so many of her hopes and dreams first became realities. Today, many travel to this site to pay tribute to her and her work as well as to be inspired to continue that work themselves.

Mother Teresa was a woman who had lived multiple lives. In her first life, she had been a school-teacher and principal. In her next life, she had started and become the leader of a successful religious order. She then took on a number of new roles once this order went international, and she became a beacon of peace throughout the world. Finally, she became an emblem of peace herself, traveling around the world and using her presence to draw attention to disasters throughout the world and the victims they produced. And yet, Mother Teresa was only human. We ought not think that she did not face any struggles of her own throughout her life. This became most apparent when, in 2003, three of her private correspondences were published, including the journals she was first asked to keep by the archbishop of Calcutta and had done so throughout her life. In these journals, one finds the intimate musings of a woman who suffered a crisis of faith, indeed for practically the last 50 years of her life. Faced with so much death and destruction, she often questioned God's plan for the world and whether He had forsaken it.

But we ought not be disheartened by this revelation—indeed, not at all. In the midst of all of her tremendous successes, it is easy to overlook Mother Teresa's humanity; it is easy to say that she was only able to achieve what she did because she was, in some way, greater than other humans. However, as her journals reveal, this was not the case. She confronted the same fears and uncertainties as anyone else does, at least at some point in their life. The commandment to love God by loving the suffering Christ in the poor of the world was something with which she thought others would struggle. It was something with which she often found herself struggling. For this reason, Mother Teresa ought to inspire us. If she carried within her soul many of the same thoughts and doubts that we do—if she was challenged to love others in the same way we often find ourselves to be challenged—then we can come to realize that her achievements are not beyond our reach. We, too, can do great things in the world, just as Mother Teresa did.

Many individuals quickly began calling Mother Teresa a saint after her death. The road to sainthood, of course, is a long one; however, hearing the calls of his people and of God, Pope John Paul II did what he could to speed up this process. Typically, one must wait five years after an individual's death before the sainthood process can begin. John Paul II, however, waived this time period in 1999, only two years after her death. Her name moved quickly through the first two steps of the process, being granted first the title of "Servant of God" and then of "Venerable."

Then, on October 19, 2003, Pope John Paul II beatified her, the third step on the road toward sainthood. This step granted her the title "Blessed" and could only come about through the recognition of a miracle. This miracle had taken place a year earlier. A woman named Monica Besra, who herself was not a Christian, had been suffering from a huge abdominal tumor. The Sisters of Charity prayed over the woman, asking

Mother Teresa to watch over and protect her. They also place a locket with a picture of Mother Teresa on her stomach at the site of the tumor. The next day, the woman woke up to find that her tumor had disappeared.

This is the most recent step in the process toward sainthood for Mother Teresa. There is one final step that requires the recognition of a second miracle. While this has not yet taken place, there is little doubt that one day it will and that Mother Teresa will officially become a modern-day saint of the Catholic Church.

# Conclusion

Mother Teresa was only a diminutive woman with a wide smile and a wrinkled face, yet she achieved greatness. She revolutionized modern Catholic missionary work. She started and led an international religious organization that served people in numerous ways throughout the world. She even brought peace to the Middle East, if only for a day. In short, she showed the world that, by re-imagining the meaning of family, people, and love, an individual could bring about peace.

In many ways, Mother Teresa's story does not end. We are still waiting for her sainthood, but her continuing story is more than just this. She serves as a role model for individuals everywhere. Her life teaches us (as she taught Muggeridge many years ago) that it is never too late to make a difference in the world. What is more, one must never be satisfied with what one has achieved but always seek out new ways in which one can achieve more. One can never do too much good in the world; one can never help too many people. Her life also teaches us that, although this task may seem daunting, especially in today's world, the first step is easy. All one needs to do is to follow in Mother Teresa's footsteps and step beyond the walls that separate one from those in need around them.

Made in the USA
Columbia, SC
19 February 2021

33235149R00157